The Cross Media Revolution: Ownership and Control

Tim Congdon, Andrew Graham,
Damian Green and Bill Robinson

John Libbey

LONDON · PARIS · ROME

British Library Cataloguing in Publication Data

A catalogue record for this book is available from the British Library.

ISBN: 0 86196 545 0

Published by

John Libbey & Company Ltd, 13 Smiths Yard, Summerley Street,
London SW18 4HR, England.
Telephone: +44 (0)181-947 2777: Fax +44 (0)181-947 2664
John Libbey Eurotext Ltd, 127 rue de la République, 92120 Montrouge, France.
John Libbey - C.I.C. s.r.l., via Lazzaro Spallanzani 11, 00161 Rome, Italy

Printed in Great Britain by Gwynprint, Hurstpierpoint, Sussex, England.

Contents

List of Tables

Foreword

It is five short years since British broadcasting ceased to be a heavily regulated duopoly. In those five years, one household in five has chosen to pay for cable or satellite services, giving them access to 30 or so television channels. We all have a real choice of radio services, with an average of 15 available to most homes. The number of independent production companies is growing.

It is an expanding world. Press and publishing interests are looking for new profit centres in the electronic media. Radio and TV companies are hungry for investment.

In the next five years, this change will accelerate. The digital revolution will cause the convergence of broadcasting, telecoms and computing technologies, creating the potential for a £20 billion business sector. Our current radio and television industry – worth some £5 billion – is small by comparison, but central. Its skills and products are judged the key to consumer interest in new services, whether niche channels, data services, video-on-demand, CD ROMs or home shopping.

The business opportunities are important. But the political implications (in the broadest cultural sense) may be even greater, since modern society is shaped, to a considerable extent, by the media available to the home and the ability of individuals to communicate with one another. No-one can be certain where these changes will lead and what their impact will be. But decisions need to be taken now about the competitive framework for this developing industry.

Government has already looked at this question three times in five years; first in the 1990 Broadcasting Act, then in the granting of a new ten year Charter for the BBC and, now, with a consultation paper[1] on media ownership. This proposes an interim set of changes to relax current ownership constraints, but without departing from the principle of limiting concentration, both within and across the constituent industry sectors of press, radio and television. For the first time, it asks whether these sectors will soon be sufficiently inter-changeable to permit future ownership limits to be set across the industry as a whole and based on one single measure of media influence.

The public response has been disappointing, perhaps because most participants have a strong business interest in the outcome. Although the White Paper did ask fundamental questions about the public interest and the role of the media in democratic and cultural life, there has been a tendency to point to obligations laid upon the BBC and other network broadcasters and to understate the ways in which the media as a whole is special.

The essays here take issue with this approach. Tim Congdon argues that Britain

---

1. CM 2872, May 1995.

is unusually fortunate in the open nature of its society. Our culture resists extremism and values critical intelligence. 'The multimedia revolution must not threaten the success of British broadcasting in nurturing cultural diversity and political pluralism.' The media is different from other industries. Its competition framework has two purposes:

- to guarantee proper competition in the economic sphere; but also

- to sustain the well-being of society through the range of information made available and the diversity of political and cultural voices carried.

Tim Congdon, Andrew Graham and Bill Robinson all argue that economic issues are best addressed through general monopoly legislation and by the existing competition authorities. Andrew Graham points out that measures of media influence are irrelevant here. There is no economic case for an industry 'exchange rate' between one media sector and another. On the contrary, introducing one would prejudge work elsewhere left to empirical investigation by the Office of Fair Trading (OFT) or MMC.

All four essays focus on a political, cultural and social need for real competition and diversity in sources of information and ideas. Tim Congdon believes that the British tradition of regulating the content of popular networks cannot survive the more competitive pressures of the multimedia world. In a future with many more, but less regulated services, there will be, if anything, a greater need for an effective, impartial BBC and for ownership rules that produce a reasonable number of commercial players.

Andrew Graham and Bill Robinson argue that it is impossible to establish a common currency by which to determine those rules. This is clear from the variety of measures already suggested and the problems with each. Andrew Graham notes that 'the variety of possible measures combined with different results, special pleading and arbitrary assumptions, make it highly unlikely that any search for a single "objective" measure will succeed'.

But the more fundamental question is whether, in principle, any measure can be objective when the ultimate concern is the political and cultural question 'What form of media industry is consistent with our democratic society'?

The authors have different perspectives, but there is a strong common theme. Society has an interest in ensuring every household has the opportunity to receive the services needed for full participation in a democratic society, developing the critical powers of individuals and informing their interests and life choices. The BBC carries a key responsibility here. But that is a necessary and not a sufficient condition of success.

It is also important to promote the widest possible distribution of a range of new and multimedia services, since competition is a driving force for diversity and innovation. Urgent attention is needed to possible pinch points in the supply chain.

The major one, clearly, is the 'gateway' through which audiences access new channels or services, involving conditional access systems, programme menus and subscriber management. Damian Green supports a proposal in the recent White Paper on Digital Terrestrial Television[2] for a licensing system to ensure that any

provider of encryption or subscription services should not be permitted to discriminate for or against service providers and should not unreasonably refuse service
providers carriage on fair terms. But he argues strongly that such a measure will only
be effective if enforced across all digital systems. Otherwise, 'if the current vertical
integration obtained by programme producers who have also gained a stranglehold
on the transponders of the Astra Satellite *and* a decisive lead in subscriber management systems, is allowed to continue unchecked, then the existence of hundreds of
channels will be irrelevant'. There will be fewer providers with *effective* access to
viewers than in the traditional, regulated broadcasting world.

Another pressure point is the capacity for cash rich operators to monopolise
scarce and highly prized programming, such as major sporting events, limiting
access and earning 'monopoly rents' from their subscribers. This tactic has already
ensured that BSkyB's cable competitors have found it was not practical to seek to
develop rival sports channels and have preferred a deal which guarantees access to
Sky Sports. Since sport is the key driver of new media services, this deal effectively
kills off the possibility of strong rival programming emerging from UK cable.

The issues raised by cross-media ownership are too varied and fundamental to
be solved by reference to one system or measure. Andrew Graham argues that just
as it is dangerous for too much power to be concentrated in the hands of one
broadcaster, so it is dangerous for a single regulator to become too powerful.
'Democracy may be better served by having different bodies standing for different
things'. Bill Robinson points out that we do not expect the Chancellor of the
Exchequer to manage the economy with reference to one indicator. Why, therefore,
should we expect to manage the business of ideas with one only?

The Government has wisely invited a longer-term debate on these issues than
can be concluded within the White Paper consultation period. The views expressed
here are those of the authors, not of the BBC, but they are published as a contribution
to a debate which the nation cannot afford to get wrong.

Patricia Hodgson*

*Patricia Hodgson is the BBC's Director of Policy and Planning. Thanks are due to David Levy, who collected
and edited these essays on behalf of the BBC.

2. CM 2946, August 1995.

Summary

T hese essays contain a range of different perspectives on the issue of media concentration. This summary highlights the most striking or controversial points, grouped by topic. It is important to emphasise that it does not, therefore, represent all the views of any individual author, nor is it a statement of a collective view of either the authors or the BBC.

1. The case for reviewing media ownership laws

- Technology is transforming the media business, promising a convergence of broadcast, print and personal forms of communication and increasing opportunities for companies to operate across previously discrete media. These changes will open up new business opportunities and raise significant economic, political and even cultural issues.

- The ending of spectrum scarcity, the growth in channels and the arrival of charging mechanisms through conditional access systems, may appear to make the media an industry like any other and thereby undermine the rationale for media specific regulation.

- But while there is a strong case for regulating the *economic* aspects of media concentration in the same way as for any other industry the importance of the media's role for democracy, as well as the role of the new digital gateways – in controlling access to, and hence choice for, the consumer – means that there will continue to be *political* grounds for a competition framework special to the media.

- This framework may need to be updated to take account of the increasing convergence between media sectors. But the proposal that there should be an integrated media 'exchange rate' based on 'objective' factors, so that different media sectors can be regulated as a total media market, is seriously flawed. Insofar as it fails to distinguish between media content with an axe to grind and that which is impartial, it compares chalk with cheese.

- Examination of a detailed range of measures of media influence reveals that none are satisfactory individually. There is no agreed set of measures to assess the political impact of the media and it is questionable whether there ever could be an 'objective' set of answers to the essentially *political* question as to what form of media industry is consistent with a democratic society.

2. Economic grounds for action

- Concerns about undue economic dominance in the media industry – about abuses of pricing power and conventional attempts to restrict entry – are very similar to those that arise in other industries and can be countered by existing competition legislation. But new threats are emerging which may require special attention, in particular the role of conditional access systems that can restrict the customers' choice of programmes and content.

- While the speed of technical change in the media adds to the complexity of the problems facing regulators, on its own it neither provides grounds on which to deal with the economic aspects of concentration in the media in a different way from that which is used for other industries, nor to establish 'exchange rates' between one media sector and another.

3. The political foundations of media regulation

- The Government was right to identify in their White Paper the unique role that television, radio and the press play in the 'free expression of ideas and opinion, and thus in the democratic process' and that the 'main objective (of public policy) must therefore be to secure a plurality of sources of information and opinion, and a plurality of editorial control over them'.

- Any proposals must first define what kind of influence should be targeted. There are two possible definitions – *political* influence in its broadest sense – affecting news, current affairs and possibly including wider cultural material – and a much broader form of *commercial* influence encompassed in the ability to pursue a corporate agenda through the print and media industries as a whole. The two forms of influence may call for differing responses.

4. A policy framework for the digital world

- The goal of public policy in the digital world must be to ensure that viewers and listeners benefit from the multimedia revolution, without threatening the success of British broadcasting in nurturing cultural diversity and political pluralism.

- While digital technology will provide an unprecedented increase in the amount of information available, and the variety of means by which it can be obtained, this will not by itself solve problems of ensuring that a plurality of viewpoints remain available. In the broadcasting world, unlike the Internet, the onset of digital technology promises to increase concentration.

- There will be a need for an effective framework to maintain diversity. Governments, either nationally or internationally, will have a legitimate role in:

  Ensuring that every household has the opportunity to receive the services needed for full participation in a democratic society. It is particularly important that the poor, who are the least likely to be able to receive subscription services, should not be cut off from well-informed news, top sport, high quality entertainment, the arts and sciences.

Promoting the widest possible distribution of new multimedia services. This must be based on the preservation of competition, as the best driving force for innovation.

Preventing the emergence of monopolies at any stage of the production and distribution chain which takes programmes into the home.

5. The importance of digital gateways

- Action will be necessary to prevent the emergence of 'gateway monopolies' by which the owners of encryption technology and subscriber management systems can squeeze out commercial rivals, and control the means of communication.

- Control of these access points, and, in particular control of the set-top boxes for televisions, may prove to be far more important than direct market dominance, both in determining access *now* and, more important, in having a critical influence on the *future shape* of the media industry.

- In the Government's Media Ownership proposals they suggest that 'gatekeepers' (i.e. conditional access points such as set-top boxes for televisions) will be controlled only through existing competition law. In addition, the Government is failing to insist that there should be common standards for these boxes.

- The damage caused by a lack of common standards will be felt first by consumers. Those who are unwilling to buy a multiplicity of set-top boxes could be dependent on only a single supplier for all their news, information and entertainment. In other words *individual* consumers could well face an undesirable concentration of media influence *even when no such concentration would be apparent at the level of the industry as a whole.*

- Since many consumers will choose only to buy a single box (or even none at all since no single box will give access to the full range of programmes), manufacturers and programme makers will face smaller markets and higher unit costs. The economic consequences of this understandable consumer response will be particularly damaging – small and unnecessarily fragmented markets will reduce choice, raise costs, lower demand and reduce investment.

- One approach would require Government to make common standards mandatory. In the media industry common standards will be the prerequisite for common carriers and common carriers will be the prerequisite for media competition and for unhindered access to information. The move to common standards could also be pursued by building on the suggestion of the ITC (of 18

July 1995) that it should draw up a code of practice on conditional access and that conditional access should be a licensable activity.

· The recently adopted European Television Standards Directive takes another approach. It obliges conditional access operators to offer access to broadcasters on fair, reasonable, and non-discriminatory terms. These principles were endorsed for digital terrestrial broadcasting in the Government's recent White Paper and it was proposed that OFTEL be given the role of licensing digital terrestrial conditional access systems. One way forward would be to extend that regime to the entire digital world.

6. A role for public broadcasters in the digital age

· In the digital age, it will be necessary to maintain a common culture and avoid increased choice leading only to cultural fragmentation. Enthusiasts for cyber-space may claim that world-wide communities of common interest will replace the geographical loyalties of the past. In practice it would be short-sighted to allow too much diminution in the ability of the existing mass media to bring communities together, to provide shared experiences, and to give all citizens the chance to seize the choices and opportunities that are available.

· The belief that the quality of information available to society as a whole is fundamental to public policy, has a long history. Adam Smith favoured universal education as a means of ensuring 'an instructed and intelligent people' who, he argued 'are always more decent and orderly than an ignorant and stupid one'. Similarly, the quality of a nation's media is vital to sustaining the plurality of debate and liberating the critical powers of the populace that Karl Popper argued were necessary for the preservation of an 'Open Society'.

· Profit-maximisation and political pluralism are different and not necessarily complementary objectives. Whereas the commercial criteria for profit maximisation apply at the level of particular businesses, the preconditions of healthy political debate are met, or not met, at the level of society as a whole. The price mechanism may secure efficiency but it should be recognised that there are areas – in the law courts (where the aim is justice), or in selecting articles for academic journals (where the aim is the furthering of knowledge) – where it is inappropriate. Similarly, a public service broadcaster can and ought to have objectives different from those of a privately-owned broadcaster.

· Excellent news coverage is essential to a nation's political culture. Just as there can be little confidence that unregulated commercial broadcasters are much concerned to maintain pluralism in political debate, so there can be no presumption that the free market will give top priority to the truthfulness of the news or seek an appropriate mix of news and other programming. There will also be a need to ensure that certain other types of programmes do not disappear from the screens of those who do not have subscription services.

· Content regulation is not the answer. Already, increased competition is making content-related rules harder to enforce. In the mature multimedia world of 20-30 years hence, they will be irrelevant. Broadcasters then must be as free as current newspaper publishers. Ironically, that freedom will make a public service broadcaster, such as the BBC, more necessary *and* put a premium on proper competition within the commercial sector. But any ownership controls devised for the digital world must be based on a clear assessment of the kind of diversity they seek to promote and of the types of influence they are directed at containing.

7. Establishing a framework for controlling media concentration

- The weakness of proposals reflected in the Government's consultation paper is that they conflate news and opinion programmes (where pluralism matters greatly) with entertainment, where it matters much less. Since news only accounts for 11 per cent of TV audiences by genre (as against 29 per cent for drama and 18 per cent for light entertainment) a company which had complete control over all news output, but very low output in other genres would emerge with a very low overall market share.

- If the policy objective is to limit the political influence of any one company, the government's proposed product market definition is much too wide. If on the other hand, the concern is for commercial influence – or the ability of an entity to pursue its own corporate agenda through, for example, cross promotion across a range of news, information and entertainment outlets – then the product market is defined too narrowly (and should include other audiovisual products such as video, cinema, magazines etc).

- Certain principles should therefore underpin the rules governing media concentration:

  The market should be defined in a way which recognises the nature of media products, as much as the means of transmission of those products. The relevant markets are thus not just the television market, the radio market and the newspaper market, but include consideration of the products transmitted by those means – the game show market, the news market, the market in political comment.

  The rules governing the markets in information and opinion should be more tightly drawn than those governing the market in entertainment. We should be more worried if a single company has 20 per cent of the market in news than we would be if it had 20 per cent of the market in game shows. The market share required to exert excessive *influence* in say, news programmes, may be less than that needed to wield excessive *market power*.

8. Measuring market shares

- The influence of any medium depends on a complex mix of factors. Among

8

them are the number of people reached; the amount of time they spend regularly absorbing the messages transmitted; the amount of money they are prepared to spend for that information; the amount of attention they pay to it when they receive it; and on who those people are – whether they are themselves influential. Some of these things are fairly easy to gauge, others are more difficult or impossible to measure.

.   All the various individual measures of media influence suffer from the following problems.

They produce radically different results. Capital Radio's impact is twelve times higher measured by its share of time spent consuming the media than if measured by revenues. Groups tend to advocate measures that minimise their influence.

They often incorporate arbitrary assumptions about the impact of differing forms of media.

.   Ultimately the judgement about the influence of any medium is qualitative. Each measure provides some information about the influence of different companies, but there is no mechanical way of combining these pieces of information into a single measure of influence.

.   Just as the Chancellor of the Exchequer receives a wide range of information to decide whether inflationary pressures are sufficient to justify a rise in interest rates, so any media regulator will need a great deal of information extracted from a wide range of indicators to help them decide if the influence of a particular company is a cause for concern.

The Multimedia Revolution and the Open Society

Tim Congdon

I Introduction

The advance of electronic technology over the last decade has opened new horizons for broadcasting and the media. As the Government's White Paper on *Media Ownership* notes, 'The dynamics of technological change carry with them the potential to reshape the nature of the media industry, and to create new business opportunities.'[1] It has also created difficult questions for public policy, with economic and political concerns intersecting in new and unexpected ways. There is a widespread recognition that, while the economic approach to regulating competition is still relevant, the multimedia revolution raises broader political and even cultural issues. At a minimum, the regulatory framework must sustain the open society. It must ensure that Britain tries to be, in Karl Popper's words, a 'society which rejects the absolute authority of the merely established and the merely traditional while trying to preserve, to develop and to establish traditions, old and new, that measure up to ... standards of freedom, of humaneness, and of rational criticism'.[2]

The impact of new technology

In this context two key aspects of the technological changes need to be highlighted. First, and most important, is that the number of potential channels for television programmes is increasing rapidly, mainly because of the introduction of satellite and cable transmission. In the early decades of television, transmission was possible only from terrestrial stations and the number of technically-feasible channels was limited (so-called 'spectrum scarcity'). This scarcity justified special treatment by government, since broadcasters' monopoly or oligopoly position might otherwise have been abused. Further, until recently viewers could not be charged for particular programmes because the billing technology did not exist.

But the necessary technology, known as 'conditional access technology' (because access to a programme is conditional on payment in some form), is now being developed. As spectrum scarcity is overcome and more suppliers are involved, and as the scope for pricing individual programmes to individual customers evolves, the structure of the media market begins to resemble that in competitive industries.

---

1. The Department of National Heritage *Media Ownership: the Government's Proposals* (London: HMSO, 1995), paragraph 5.17, p. 19.

2. K. R. Popper *The Open Society and its Enemies* (London: Routledge & Kegan Paul, 5th ed., 1966), vol. 1, p. ix.

The argument for special treatment is therefore increasingly obsolete. In particular, the original case for a dominant public service broadcaster (i.e. the BBC) financed by a licence fee is less compelling.

The second is that the gap between 'publication' (of print in newspapers, magazines and books) and 'broadcasting' (of audio or audio-visual material on television and radio) is being bridged, so that new means of disseminating material blend features of both publication and broadcasting. This is most obvious with screen-based information services, such as Reuters and Bloomberg, which can convey text, graphics or pictures, depending on the customers' wishes. Indeed, in the new world now emerging it is uncertain in some contexts whether 'publication' or 'broadcasting' is the right word to use, and the neologism 'narrowcasting' has been coined. Ultimately televisions and personal computers may become indistinguishable.

Commercial responses

One commercial response to these changes is that companies have begun to operate in several different types of media. They may have interests in newspapers and television (or in newspapers and radio, or whatever), and in television they can participate in terrestrial stations as well as satellite and cable. By spanning several media, valuable advantages are obtained in production and marketing. In the words of the *Media Ownership* White Paper, 'new technology is permitting a single piece of intellectual property to be exploited many times over, in different geographical and product markets'.[3] The benefits in production are obvious, that substantially the same artistic and intellectual performances can be packaged for several media instead of only one. The gains in marketing are more complex. Apart from the ability to label a product with a well-known brand name and to publish or broadcast it, with only slight amendment, through a number of distinct media outlets, there is also scope to advertise in one type of media a product which has already appeared in another.

II Questions for public policy

The rationale for restrictions on cross-media holdings

The first question for public policy is 'should cross-media ownership be restricted and, if so, by how much and according to what criteria?'. In some ways excessive concentration in the media industries raises similar concerns for public policy to those arising from excessive concentration in any industry. Most obviously, there are dangers that pricing power will be abused and new entry restricted, and that – because of the consequent absence of new competition – suppliers will become lazy and inefficient. But these dangers are present in all areas of the economy and can be countered by existing monopoly legislation. Perhaps the only important economic respect in which the media industries differ from others is that much of their revenue comes from advertising instead of purely from sales to customers. As a result the revenues of the media industries are not a reliable measure of the benefits that viewers, listeners and readers receive. It follows that, even from an entirely econ-

---

3. *Media Ownership*, p. 19.

omic standpoint, there are special problems in determining the socially optimal level of media output.

The political implications of media concentration

The focus here will be on the political, not the economic, aspects of undue concentration in cross-media ownership. The use of the word 'political' must not be understood too narrowly. The output of the media industries can profoundly affect a society's well-being in ways which can be assessed neither by counting revenues, costs and profits, nor by measuring the vitality of 'politics' in the conventional sense. Performances in the media affect such varied aspects of national life as dress codes, religious beliefs, sentiments of patriotism (or anti-patriotism) and so on. At least potentially, undue concentration in cross-media ownership might lead to an over-enthusiasm for particular religious beliefs, to extremes of sexual licence or puritanism, and to excesses of approval or disapproval of particular forms of dress, among other things.

In the British context references to religious and moral fanaticism may seem far-fetched. But life in many other countries is blighted by the prevalence of extremes (of political or religious belief, and the associated codes of dress and personal mores), and typically the media are involved in imposing and enforcing these extremes on individuals. Britain is a fortunate nation. Not only does it enjoy high living standards and a healthy political democracy, but also it suffers hardly at all from such imposed extremes. Instead it creates a wide range of cultural and intellectual products which stimulate individuals to think for themselves and respect other individuals' beliefs. An open society of course resists political tyranny and is indeed suspicious of any form of political extremism. But it must also somehow nurture diversity and pluralism in art, culture and morality.[4]

By common consent, the freedom of individual expression in Britain is exceptional compared with most other nations. The importance of the BBC in maintaining the vitality of Britain's political and cultural life is a matter of debate. But Britain must have got something right, and perhaps the structure of its broadcasting and media industries has played a part. Public policy has to ensure that viewers and listeners benefit from the multimedia revolution, but at the same time the multimedia revolution must not threaten the success of British broadcasting in nurturing cultural diversity and political pluralism. The questions become, 'what structure of media regulation and ownership, including cross-media ownership, lends most support to the institutions of the open society?' and 'what should be the role of public service broadcasting in the new world of extensive cross-media ownership?'.

The central argument will be that a public service broadcaster such as the BBC can make a special contribution to preserving the institutions of the open society. The first stage in the argument will be to describe the conditions of healthy political

---

4. 'In many Asian countries, the television industry is also subject to additional controls for many political and ideological reasons, not least of which has been the desire to block transmissions of programmes deemed unsuitable to the culture, religious beliefs or sensibilities of the nation's ruling elite and, by extension, to their populations. In the short-term, this reinforces the profit position of those lucky enough to hold licences.' B. Sturgess *Global Television: Focus on Asia* (London: Barings Research, 1995), p.32.

debate and to show that, left to themselves, commercial interests are unlikely to be much interested in meeting these conditions.

III The conditions for healthy political debate

The role of the media in the open society

In chapter 10 of *The Open Society and its Enemies* Popper described how the struggle between Athens and Sparta in ancient Greece was not merely military and diplomatic, but was also conducted on a philosophical plane between two competing conceptions of society. Sparta represented 'the magical or tribal or collectivist society' which 'will also be called the closed society' and Athens (or at any rate certain factions in Athenian public life) 'the society in which individuals are confronted with personal decisions, the open society'.[5] The emergence of modern civilisation consisted, essentially, in the triumph of the open society over the closed society. The acceptance of individual responsibility (and so of such notions as personal freedom and private property) is possible in the open society 'in which men have learned to be to some extent critical of taboos, and to base decisions on the authority of their own intelligence (after discussion)'.[6] The open society 'sets free the critical powers of man'.

To sustain the open society the structure of the media must therefore, at a minimum, liberate these 'critical powers'. By its nature criticism assumes a bench-mark for making judgements and implies that judgements are to be made between alternatives. So political criticism, if it is to be at all meaningful, requires that there be two or more points of view. The plurality of views must be defended in an open society. In words attributed to Voltaire, 'I disapprove of what you say, but I will defend to the death your right to say it.'

The conventions of debate

A number of conventions are recognised as being essential if political debate is to be balanced, and yet to be appropriately lively and pluralist. The most basic is that every individual has the right to express his (or her) own opinion, and that every individual's opinion has some worth. An obvious correlative is that every individual has the right of reply, if an attack is made on his position. In a debate where the right to reply is often exercised, participants quickly realise that there are two or more opinions about most subjects. A further convention is therefore that everyone has the right to seek a second (or third) opinion, in order that debates can be seen 'from all sides of the question'.

These three conventions – that all individuals have the right to express their own position, the right of reply to an attack on that position and the right to seek a second opinion – must be respected if a plurality of views is to be maintained. Respect for these conventions is in fact deeply entrenched in British public life. For example, newspapers have leader pages, where the editor can state a view, and letters pages, which enable offended parties to complain about content, readers to set out their opinions and so on. These fora of opinion are not part of any written

5. Popper *Open Society* vol. 1, p. 173.
6. Popper *Open Society* vol, 1, p. 202.

constitution, but an attempt by government or commercial interests to suppress them would be a constitutional outrage. Respect for the conventions of debate is certainly part of the ethos of British broadcasting, including the ethos of the BBC.

But the word 'right' needs to be pinned down more precisely. The rights to express an opinion, to reply and to seek another opinion are not absolute, but have to be set in context. There are difficult problems of procedure. First, some issues are genuinely political and any of a whole host of opinions may be a valid component of debate. But on other issues there may be a technically correct answer which can be determined by 'experts'. All individuals may have an equal right to express an opinion, but that does not mean that all opinions are equal.

Secondly, even leaving aside the problem of technical expertise, debates must be organised in a fair and even-handed manner. Again, all individuals may have an equal right to express an opinion, but everyone taking part in a particular debate must express that right equally. They must not win, or try to win, arguments by being noisier and more loud-mouthed than their opponents. Filibustering may be an abuse of free speech, not an example of free speech taken to its extreme. There has to be a way of giving more time and space to majority views, without quelling the legitimate statement of minority positions.

Evidently, pluralism in political debate requires umpires. The umpires' task is to decide – among other matters – when a particular question is technical (to be decided by experts) rather than political (when a wide range of divergent opinions should be sought), and to determine the right balance between the time and space allowed for the various positions involved. The umpire has to be impartial and, indeed, has to be prepared to override his own political beliefs for the sake of 'fair play'. Ideally, participants and observers in political debates should not even be aware that the umpire has a personal view of his own.

IV Profit-maximisation and political pluralism are different objectives

Profits and pluralism

The discussion so far has tried to identify certain features of healthy political debate and, in particular, to define the conditions required to protect pluralism of views and outlooks in political debate. One point is surely obvious. It has been very difficult to introduce commercial criteria in the discussion. There is no evident connection between the conditions for pluralistic political debate and the motivations of companies trying to maximise their profits in a competitive environment. Does a broadcaster who always allows a right of reply, with all that may entail for programming times and a possible loss of professionalism in presentation, maximise his profits? Is a television network which selects its experts carefully and ensures they are impartial likely to improve its bottom line? Can it make commercial sense to give worthy minorities a chance, in view of the probable indifference of most viewers and the resulting slide in the ratings?

The view being set out here must not be misinterpreted. The claim is emphatically not that the free market economy is likely to suppress political debate. On the contrary, the institution of private property and the wide dispersion of private property throughout society enhance personal freedom. The point is merely that the determinants of maximum profits are on a different plane from the preconditions of healthy political debate. The commercial criteria for profit maximisation apply at the level of particular businesses, whereas the preconditions of healthy political debate are met, or not met, at the level of society as a whole. It is altogether right that the top executives of media companies should be concerned mostly to maximise their profits and not to bother themselves unduly about airy-fairy political notions. As Keynes said, it is better that businessmen tyrannise over their bank balances than over their fellow citizens. But the structure of the industry in which media executives work has a profound relevance for the nature of political debate. It is the task of others to ensure that the legitimate pursuit of private commercial ends does not undermine the open society.

Pluralism and public service broadcasting

An argument could be made that, just as free choice is extended by a wide dispersion of private property, so political pluralism is encouraged by a diversity of competing media outlets. By extension, political pluralism is helped if there are a variety of methods of paying for these outlets. The economic case for a licence fee to finance a public service broadcaster such as the BBC is undoubtedly weakened by the multimedia revolution and the overcoming of spectrum scarcity. But a new and essentially political case can be urged. In particular, a public service broadcaster can try to respect, or even perhaps to nurture, the conditions for a healthy and pluralistic political debate. Whereas a commercial media company has to put profits first, a public service broadcaster can pursue other objectives, including the objective of providing a neutral but technically expert forum for the discussion of political issues.

In this role it has clear advantages compared with a profit-seeking, private-sector company. Where it is entirely owned by the Government, it is immune to take-over; if some private shareholding is allowed, a blocking 'golden share' can be held by the Government and the same immunity can be maintained. Its journalists need therefore not feel intimidated by management and proprietors, or required to adjust their political statements to meet the proprietors' wishes, as has sometimes happened in British newspapers. The public service broadcaster can also – subject of course to the constraints of its resources – recruit well-informed specialist journalists (to decide when an issue is technical instead of political, and to select the right outside experts) and adopt the role of umpire in political debates. By contrast, for a commercial media company a large cadre of specialist journalists, who really 'know their subjects' and have to be paid well, is a costly overhead. Moreover, when it comes to reporting and analysing issues which affect their own profits, privately-owned media companies are unlikely to be objective. But a public sector broadcaster with non-market funding can try to present all sides of the case.

Again, the argument should not be misunderstood. It is certainly not a criticism of the price system or competitive market mechanisms. In many areas of social interaction the price system secures the most efficient and best result, and is undoubtedly ideal. But the price system is not used in law courts (where the aim is justice, not efficiency), or in selecting articles for academic journals (where the aim is the furthering of knowledge, not profits), or in choosing the hierarchy of the Church of England (where the concern is simply to find good men) or in many other walks of life. To say that a public service broadcaster can have – and indeed ought to have – objectives different from those of a privately-owned company is not in any way to denounce the price system, private ownership or competitive markets. Rather it is to recognise that the open society is most likely to be preserved if people look over and above market forces, and understand that the right structure of a nation's media industries is a political as well as an economic matter.

V The special importance of the news

A public service broadcaster may not have to maximise profits in the same way as a private-sector company, but it still has to keep its expenditure in line with its revenues. In some respects the cost of sustaining healthy political debate ought not to be particularly significant. Political commentary, interviews with politicians and even full-scale debates in a studio are not expensive to produce. Documentaries on political subjects are a somewhat different matter, especially if there is an international aspect, as the costs then escalate because of plane fares, translators and so on. But the real problems come in two other areas. The first, and the most important, is the news. The second is the production of 'classics' which are part of British culture, including – even if apparently at several removes – its political culture.

The importance of impartiality

All news reporting contains political value judgements and bias. This may seem a shocking statement, but it ought not to be controversial. Of the virtual infinity of reports that could be made about the state of the world in any day, only a tiny fraction constitutes 'the news' in the usually received sense. The filtering process can only work if a few items are selected and a vast mass of material excluded, and the criteria for selecting some things and excluding others already imply a political standpoint. But, if the news are necessarily subjective in practice, they ought in theory to be 'as objective as possible'. Moreover, even though often conveyed in only a few minutes, they must try to be comprehensive, to cover 'everything really important' in the world at the time in question. They are plainly a most unusual kind of broadcasting. In effect, the conventions of political debate are inverted. The news are supposed to be reported in such a way that no one involved expresses his own view, to be so impartial that no viewer, listener or reader wants to exercise a right of reply, and to be so accurate that there is no need to seek a second opinion. More concisely, the news are meant to be 'the truth' or, at any rate, as close an approximation to the truth as can be imagined. Thus purified, the news are essential input to partisan politics where many viewpoints are represented and the conventions of debate have to be respected.

In the production of news in this sense the British media are generally regarded as the world leaders. By common consent news provided by the BBC, including the World Service, is good, even excellent. But the production of news is costly. The market does work to a degree here, because viewers, listeners and readers require accuracy and truthfulness, and are more likely to follow a news service when they know it has these qualities. But there is still unlikely to be a strong link between, on the one hand, the accuracy and truthfulness of a news service and, on the other, the revenue that would be commercially made available to it in a media industry driven purely by market forces. There is evidence, for example, that the bulk of the television audience choose their preferred channel for an evening's viewing because of programmes other than the news, partly because the news takes up only a small part of the time. They do not choose a channel because it has excellent news coverage. Around a half of the viewers to the main channels' news programmes tend therefore to be 'inherited' from other programmes.

The costs of maintaining a comprehensive news service

But excellent news coverage is essential to a nation's political culture. How, then, should it be paid for? The cost of the BBC's news operations is over £120 million a year, with the average cost of an hour of television news exceeding £50,000. The BBC has reporters and correspondents in 51 places around the world, of which 27 are fully-fledged international bureaux.[7] It could reasonably claim to be the biggest news gathering operation in the world, although much depends on how the 'news' (as opposed to data collection and dissemination) is defined. (Reuters and other tape and electronic news services are, on some definitions, rather larger.) Left to themselves, commercial broadcasters would decide the balance between news coverage and the remainder of their programming by the profit criterion; a public service broadcaster can instead try to provide a news service that is both comprehensive and accurate. Just as there can be little confidence that unregulated commercial broadcasters are much concerned to maintain pluralism in political debate, so there can be no presumption that the free market will give top priority to the truthfulness of the news or seek an appropriate mix of news and other programming.

VI 'Classics' and the open society

The second costly kind of broadcasting that needs to be mentioned here is of classics of British culture which have latent political importance. As already emphasised, the open society is defined not merely by the vitality of its political debate, where 'political' has a narrow party-political meaning. The open society depends also on a host of seemingly non-political institutions which are in fact basic to intellectual and cultural pluralism, and are essential if individuals are to exercise their critical faculties to the full. Our perceptions of these institutions, and our understanding of what they do and why they should be valued, come from conversations, reading, visits to the theatre and, of course, watching television and listening to radio. The works of all the major British authors and playwrights over the centuries not only define our culture and its traditions. They also sustain attitudes of questioning towards that culture and those traditions, attitudes which are surely crucial to the open society.

Whether the BBC should make a particular effort to dramatise such works in the interests of 'national culture', even where such dramatisation could not be commercially justified, is a moot point. There are wider questions about the extent of public subsidy for the arts. But two comments seem apposite. First, where drama programmes ('soap operas') can be produced profitably on a commercial basis, the

---

7. Information supplied to the author by the BBC.

case for public subsidy via the licence fee is hardly persuasive. Secondly, many apparently non-political intellectual productions have in fact been more effective in protecting the open society than overtly political action. Consider, for example, the power of works by Swift and Orwell. Their dramatisation would probably be unappealing to a commercial broadcaster, but can be readily defended on the long-term grounds that they help the open society. There is no simple criterion for determining what resources a public service broadcaster should devote to the production of such classics, but a case of some sort can certainly be made.

VII Controlling costs and encouraging quality

Defining the scope and obligations of public service broadcasters

The political case for public service broadcasting developed in the last few paragraphs is rather fuzzy. Commercial interests, left to themselves, may not commit resources specifically to the promotion of a lively and diverse political culture, and they may under-provide resources for news coverage. So a public service broadcaster such as the BBC may legitimately have a special role. But what amount of resources should be committed by the BBC to political analysis and commentary, to the news and to the classics? How should it balance the control of costs against maintaining quality? Can the BBC be given benchmarks (of quality, impartiality and technical efficiency) so that it knows when it has failed or succeeded?

To ask these questions is to hint at the need for a body which might set benchmarks of performance and report on the BBC's success in meeting them. Such a body would have to be non-political, but nevertheless ultimately accountable to Parliament. It might give the BBC guidelines on the resourcing and content of political broadcasting, acknowledging the limitations imposed by licence fee revenue and of course ensuring editorial freedom. The body ought to pay particular attention to promoting the heterogeneity of political broadcasting at the BBC, since a variety of broadcasts would help diversity and pluralism. If the BBC is to keep a privileged position (in terms of its funding) so that it can stimulate political debate, its political broadcasting must not be monolithic, undifferentiated and drab. In its task of monitoring diversity, cost efficiency and so on, the outside body would be analogous to the regulator of the privately-owned utilities.

The onset of choice : the US experience

Experience in countries with only limited public service broadcasting suggests that political broadcasting is driven out by more banal types of programme. In the old technological environment with spectrum scarcity the pressure on television channels was to standardise progamming to meet mass tastes, in line with a theoretical prediction made in a famous article by Hotelling in 1929.[8] In the USA the diversity of television programmes was less than in the UK, despite the USA's greater resources and much larger media market. In particular, political broadcasting was less interesting and news coverage, particularly the coverage of news outside the USA, was widely regarded as weak.[9] As the multimedia revolution proceeds, the

---

8. H. Hotelling 'Stability in competition', *Economic Journal*, 1929, vol. 39, pp. 41–52.

9. Of course, these remarks reflect the author's cultural bias. They are opinions, not scientific proofs.

diversity of channels and programmes in the USA has improved dramatically. Meanwhile the international success of CNN, the news broadcaster, has been impressive. Indeed, a case has been made that 'American television features a greater variety of programme choice than anywhere else in the world. Not only does this include an astonishing quantity of and variety of entertainment programming, with more channels and longer programming hours, but also that claimed as the special province of public service broadcasting (PSB) – that is, news, public affairs and minority interest television'.[10] The cogency of this case is strengthened by the undoubted fact that locally produced news has become more abundant in the USA with the spread of cable and satellite transmission.

The greater differentiation of American media output that has accompanied the multimedia revolution is no great surprise. Television's contribution to the quality of political debate may have become more substantial than it was before. It would clearly be preposterous to claim that the structure of the USA's media industries threatens the open society. However, if American experience in the multimedia era has somewhat weakened the case for public service broadcasting, it has not invalidated concern about excessive concentration in the media industries. Like the comparable authorities in the UK, the US Federal Communications Commission would become suspicious of undue concentration of news and public affairs broadcasting in the hands of only one or a handful of companies. The argument here has been merely that, if a public service broadcaster is given a specific responsibility to provide healthy public debate and high-quality news, healthy public debate and high-quality news are more likely to be provided than if there were no public service broadcasting at all.

Public service broadcasting in an age of choice

It has to be conceded that a highly-concentrated media industry might be much more efficient, in an economic sense, than an atomistic media industry in transmitting news and public affairs programmes. Of course, if there were two or three companies dominating news and public affairs broadcasting, the number of journalists needed, and so the cost of employing them, would be less than if there were dozens of such companies. But arguably this is a situation where resource efficiency conflicts with the politically desirable. The vitality of political debate may benefit from there being a multiplicity of small rival programme makers and these rival programme makers could work for a great number of private companies. There is no particular public-policy interest in having highly differentiated soap operas, but there is considerable public-policy interest in having highly-differentiated political broadcasts.

Alternatively, a public service broadcaster could be required, by statute, to encourage the honesty, transparency and diversity of political debate. Its costs and technical efficiency should, of course, be monitored, with a body such as the proposed Public Service Broadcasting Council[11] perhaps having a role. A hybrid

10. Raymond B. Gallagher 'American television: fact and fantasy', pp. 178 – 207, in Cento Veljanovski (ed.) *Freedom in Broadcasting* (London: Institute of Economic Affairs, 1989). The quotation is from p. 179 and p. 181.

11. See the Peacock Report *Report of the Committee on Financing the BBC*, Cm 9284 (London: HMSO, 1986).

solution – with large companies co-existing with specialist small companies and a public service broadcaster (or broadcasters) – might be best of all for maintaining the lively political culture which is part of an open society. It is unlikely that high levels of concentration in the media industries, with the newspapers, television and radio under the control of a small number of companies, are the right answer.

VIII 'Content regulation' and public service broadcasting

The impact of multimedia

In the long run – as the structure of the 'electronic publishing' industry becomes similar to that of traditional publishing and, indeed, as electronic and traditional publishing unify into a single industry – it must surely be desirable that legal restrictions on content become much the same for the two types of publishing. The need for parity of treatment was one theme of the Peacock Report and has been noted by other commentators, notably Peter Jay. In Jay's words, in an open society like Britain's, newspaper publishing is largely free from official interference, and enjoys 'the basic freedom to publish, to create a new publication, to contain in it any material whatsoever within the general laws of blasphemy, libel, national security and race relations, etc.'[12] Once the multimedia revolution is complete, surely electronic publishing should have the same 'basic freedom to publish'.

Such parity of treatment could have, at least potentially, quite drastic implications for the electronic media's attitude towards political broadcasting. Newspapers are free to have a political view, including a view that it openly partisan in the party or ideological sense. But until now television and radio have in Britain not had the same freedom. They are expected to be neutral in their political coverage, because – according to the White Paper on *Media Ownership* – there is 'a continuing need to enforce impartiality of news and current affairs programmes'.[13] It would at present be regarded as highly improper for the BBC or ITN to recommend viewers to vote for a particular politician or party. Can this restriction, which works whilst the networks and ITN are dominant largely because television news and current affairs journalists impose self-censorship, survive a move to a multimedia world? And should it?

Deregulating content?

There is a clear case, in twenty to thirty years time, in a mature multimedia world where the dramatic technological upheavals are complete, for commercial television broadcasting to be as free to take a political line as newspapers are at present. But the same surely cannot be said of a public service broadcaster. Content regulation – regulation which specifies certain quality requirements and the number of hours a channel should devote to a particular kind of programme – continues to make sense in television and radio for the time being. But officially-imposed guidance on newspapers' contents would be condemned on all sides as a political abomination.

In the end content regulation in television must go. It has already been largely

---

12. See the article 'Electronic publishing', pp. 219-36, in P. Jay *The Crisis for Western Political Economy and Other Essays* (London: Andre Deutsch, 1984).

13. *Media Ownership*, HMSO, paragraph 4.8, p. 13.

abandoned in Italy and the Netherlands. In the USA also the so-called 'fairness doctrine', by which the FCC required broadcasters to cover controversial issues in local politics and imposed the obligation to offer a right to reply, has been attacked by the US Supreme Court.[14] However, in the UK content regulation may need to last longer than in the USA, not least because it is a smaller country and the risk of a too dominant media group is therefore greater. Already the intensification of commercial pressures is starting to dilute the British media's traditional commitment to prominent, high-quality news programmes. In 1994 the independent television companies wanted to move *News at Ten* to a different slot, away from the peak time for advertising revenues, and were prevented from doing so only by the Independent Television Commission.

Moreover, without some restrictions on ownership, the ending of content regulation would renew the original problem, that – if large multimedia groups cornered a high proportion of the market in television, newspapers and radio, and if they were no longer constrained by such regulation – all the key forms of media could be disfigured by biased or extremist politics. Even if extremism were somehow prevented, certain television and radio channels could become obviously 'left-wing' or 'right-wing', and might increasingly disrespect the conventions of healthy public debate. (Indeed, the FCC's decision to allow companies to refuse a right to reply is interesting.)

A case can be made that the ending of content regulation in commercial broadcasting ought therefore to be accompanied by the deliberate reinforcement of public service broadcasting. Public service broadcasting could be subject to an official remit to respect the conventions of public debate, to nurture political pluralism and to keep the news accurate. In this way the adoption of clearly political standpoints by commercial television and radio would not prevent viewers, readers and listeners from receiving the impartial and balanced political coverage to which in Britain they have become accustomed. A public service broadcaster such as the BBC, with its funding almost immune to political meddling, would act as a counterweight to a particularly opinionated media company or group in private hands. So, in a curious way, the existence of the BBC could help the full liberation of political broadcasting in the commercial sector. The BBC and the rest of the media industry might actually have an interest in common. To play this public-interest role, the BBC's financing may need to come – to a large degree – from non-market sources.

IX Conclusion: the multimedia revolution can strengthen the open society

The open society depends on the untrammelled ability of large numbers of free but responsible individuals to exercise their critical powers to the full. The multimedia revolution ought to strengthen the open society. By increasing many fold the number of media outlets, it ought to expand individuals' opportunities to express themselves and to participate in public debate. Further, the range of media output ought to become more diverse and more interesting. The quality of political debate ought to

---

14. Gallagher in *Freedom in Broadcasting*, p. 198–199.

improve, whether the term 'political debate ' is understood in either a narrow party-political sense or a broader cultural context.

But there have to be worries that these gains will be forfeited if the media industries are too highly concentrated in a small number of privately-owned companies. Shareholders and managements are concerned, very properly, with maximising their profits, not with larger questions of public policy such as the need to sustain a healthy political debate. The multimedia revolution plainly casts doubt on the original rationale for the BBC's licence fee, which depended on spectrum scarcity. However, the case has been argued here for the retention of a public service broadcaster like the BBC with a specific responsibility for providing high-quality news, offering a forum for debates about key issues of public policy and protecting certain conventions about the right conduct of such debates. This role would have resource costs, and the BBC would of course have to operate efficiently and within budget. But it could give priority to such ends as the diversity and fairness of the debate, and not concentrate on profits alone. The continuance of the BBC's obligation to be fair and transparent in its political broadcasting might make it easier to end the regulation of political content in the commercial sector. As electronic and print publishing converge, control over political content in television and radio programmes will become increasingly unacceptable.

The argument developed in this paper should not be misunderstood and it should not be pressed too far. As already emphasised, it is not in any way intended as an attack on the free market, the price mechanism or private property. It has also to be conceded that the presence of a dominant public service broadcaster may inhibit the developments of new, small and dynamic media companies, simply because so much of the existing market is held by the BBC. To some extent this danger can be overcome if the BBC is required to take a certain proportion of its output from the independent sector, as is already the case. In this context one point needs to be heavily emphasised: in the international arena the BBC is itself subject to competition from large and well- capitalised rivals. Its much-admired past makes it the ideal candidate to become 'newscaster to the world' when the new technologies are mature and widely installed across the globe. But it could fulfil that ambition only were it ultimately to develop sources of revenue separate from, and much more substantial than, the licence fee.

The Peacock Report's originality lay in its insistence that, in the long run, consumer sovereignty ought to prevail in broadcasting and the media, just as it does in other areas of the economy. But broadcasting is different from other industries in a very fundamental way. Broadcasting does not merely offer products to meet known and fairly fixed consumer preferences; it also presents cultural and intellectual products which themselves mould people's preferences. Because they disseminate much of the political reporting and analysis found in Britain, media companies have a powerful effect on the terms and nature of political debate. When the multimedia revolution is complete, people may receive input to their political thinking from many different sources. But at present even in multi-channel homes 70 per cent of viewing is of the main terrestrial networks and polls cite television as the prime source of news for 70 per cent of the population.

Public policy can legitimately override market forces if, by so doing, it defends an open society in which the idea of free choice is respected. High levels of concentration in the media might reduce the diversity of the inputs to the political debate and, to that degree, weaken the open society. As the multimedia revolution takes hold over the next 20 or 30 years, some mix of public service and commercial broadcasting may be better than a purely market outcome in maintaining Britain's democratic culture.

Preserving Plurality in a Digital World

Damian Green

I Introduction: the digital future

It is vital for a modern liberal democracy that the great majority of citizens have access to a wide range of voices and opinions. For a citizen to exercise the democratic right of choosing his rulers, it is necessary that a sufficient range of information and comment is available. Otherwise choice is meaningless.

This is why the onset of the digital revolution caused by the convergence of telecommunications, broadcasting, and computers to form the so-called 'information superhighway'(a bad and misleading analogy; what is being created is a network, not a linear highway) is a cause of excitement in political circles across the spectrum. Some believe that the ability to access unlimited information in the home *and* to express an instant decision based on that information will transform democratic government completely, removing much of the need for representative institutions and moving the world closer to direct democracy.

Whether that particular path is either realistic or desirable is outside the scope of this essay. It will deal with the question, what kind of regulation, if any, is needed for the digital world, when its participants may have started out as broadcasters, phone companies, on-line services, or some completely new animal.

The new digital world

The outline of the digital world is already apparent. It contains a multiplicity of TV channels, increasing use of telephone lines for new services, including data and video transmission, and the increasing versatility of personal computers (PCs) with links through modems to entertainment and information throughout the world. The speed of development has already been extraordinary, and the pace of change is accelerating. Less than ten years ago Britain had four TV channels. Even before digital TV arrives millions of homes can receive several dozen channels and within the next year or so digital services will start offering hundreds of channels. One piece of analysis, by Inteco, suggests that the number of UK homes with a PC, currently around 21 per cent, will nearly double by 1998. CD-ROMs only became widely commercially available in 1993. Already more than half a million homes have a CD-ROM drive, and Inteco expects this to rise to 3.5 million by 1998. Others project much faster growth both for CD-ROM drives and modems, because PCs will increasingly include them as standard features.

The most breathtaking growth has been the development of the Internet, and its more commercial, multimedia offspring the World Wide Web. The Net, as a rule of thumb, doubles in size every year. No-one can guess accurately at how many users there are worldwide, but it is more than 20 million. The Web, which has now attracted the attention of the world's biggest corporations as an essential medium for sales and advertising, is growing in size at the rate of 50 per cent per month. The number of sites on the Web doubles every 53 days, according to Sun Microsystems.

A contrast is often drawn with the old world, where 'spectrum' was a scarce resource protected by Governments, and allocated only to those prepared to use it in ways approved by regulators. The conventional model for the new world of electronic media is the magazine market, where no restrictions (apart from those on libel and serious obscenity) are necessary, and every conceivable viewpoint, hobby, and taste can find a willing supplier.

Attitudes to change

Inevitably, this growth in the technical potential of electronic communications has led to talk of a revolution, which will transform all our lives. Every decade has a magazine which at the time celebrates its obsessions, proclaiming them as new but immutable truths and guides to life. Subsequently such claims look dated, and either quaint or embarrassing, according to taste. The 1960s had *Playboy* (sex), the 1970s *Rolling Stone* (rock), the 1980s *The Face* (style) and the 1990s has *Wired* (computers).

Like its predecessors in their heydays, *Wired* is a brilliant creation, written by enthusiasts with a burning conviction that what they are saying is both right and important. Its philosophy is that everything is changed so radically by the onset of digital technology that all previous means of communication and control are irrelevant. Hence, the only attitude for regulatory authorities in the new world is to get out of the way. To quote from the first UK edition of *Wired*, earlier this year:

> The Digital Revolution is whipping through our lives like a Bengali typhoon- while the mainstream media is still groping for the snooze button...The most fascinating and powerful people today are not politicians or priests, or generals or pundits, but the vanguard who are integrating digital technologies into their business and personal lives, and causing social changes so profound their only parallel is probably the discovery of fire.

On this view of the future, all the old institutions such as Parliament and the BBC are set to lose power to the individual, and the interesting political divide is not between Left and Right (*Wired* is scathing about all parties in this country, and attracted to Newt Gingrich because of his enthusiasm for the Net) but between authoritarians and meritocrats.

It would of course be an enormous boon if technology could solve the problems of education, public representation, mass entertainment and worldwide cultural exchange. It is an updated capitalist version of Karl Marx's vision for the ultimate purpose of socialism, the withering away of the state. As such, it is enormously attractive. Serious questions, though, are in order about how realistic it is.

In particular, over the next decade, when the growth of digital communications will be amazingly fast, but before it is possible to judge the full consequences of this growth, would it be right to jettison the traditional institutions that have attempted to ensure diversity and pluralism? It seems extremely likely that fibre optics and modems will be of much greater long-term value to society than pictures of naked bunny girls, 20-minute drum solos, and sharp suits, all of which came recommended as significant signs of progress by *Wired*'s predecessors. That is no reason to assume that new delivery systems will automatically free societies from having to ensure that contrasting views can be delivered.

The model of the Internet up to now has been that of individual providers and consumers, exchanging information on a relatively free and casual basis. That model is already changing with the increasingly businesslike nature of the Web. In the field of broadcasting, developments have moved in the opposite direction. The chain of business, from programme-makers to viewers, has become highly integrated, with a small number of huge world-wide players dominating the industry. So even if the broadcasting world expands it is unlikely to become more like the Internet, where ease of entry is a notable feature. Therefore it is right to question whether simple libertarian solutions are the best way of preserving diversity of opinion and comment.

II Necessary regulation in the digital world

Arguments for an end to controls

Those who believe that the end of spectrum scarcity (which is what digital compression and transmission technologies promise) should signal the end of Government involvement in broadcasting regulation advance three arguments.

The first is that regulation will become unnecessary. The monopoly power of the old networks has been destroyed by the advent of new TV and radio channels, which have allowed a range of voices on to the air that were kept off beforehand. The digital world will have hundreds of traditional TV channels, as well as information delivery over phone lines that will contain elements of traditional TV such as up-to-date information and moving pictures. These will arrive either on a PC or the TV screen. So there will be less need to ensure balanced and fair access to viewers. Power will have been transferred from the regulator and the broadcaster to the viewer.

The second argument is that regulation will become ineffective. This issue is particularly acute on the Internet, where instant international communication between individuals can now include far more than a traditional phone call, since it can involve the transmission of large amounts of text, and increasing amounts of video and audio material.

The current problems facing Governments all over the world in regulating child pornography, incitements to violence and messages from terrorist groups are, it is said, just the first signs that the Internet will simply be out of anyone's control. Unless every Government in the world agrees a regulatory code, which is impossible to imagine given, for example, the different attitudes to sexually explicit material even among the democracies, then an Internet provider thwarted in one jurisdiction will simply move to a more liberal one, in the knowledge that his message will reach around the globe.

A lesser version of the same argument is applied to satellite TV. With footprints that extend beyond national boundaries, international broadcasts can be made into countries which censor their domestic news, or which have stricter moral codes than their neighbours. In practice, this has not been the case. The British Government prevented the broadcast of a hard-core pornographic channel based in Holland and then Denmark by stopping the sale of decoders. More notoriously, the Chinese Government made it clear to Rupert Murdoch that his commercial interests in the world's biggest potential market would be harmed if his Star satellite continued carrying BBC news broadcasts. So Mr Murdoch replaced them with a film channel.

The third argument against regulation which has been prominent in the UK has been an industrial one, based on the thesis that only the big will flourish as convergence accelerates, and that national restrictions designed to prevent monopolies disadvantage domestic companies who wish to compete in the world market. So competition rules should be relaxed to allow multimedia conglomerates to form, otherwise the national voice will be swamped by outsiders who have been allowed to build up a wide range of services.

Reasons for continued regulation

All of these arguments have been over-stated by their proponents, mainly for perfectly obvious (and honourable) reasons of commercial self-interest. The Government was right to take the cautious steps towards deregulation of the media market it announced in the White Paper *Media Ownership – The Government's Proposals* published in May 1995. These allow all but the biggest newspaper groups to own one or two terrestrial TV licenses, and allow TV companies to buy newspaper interests. There are also relaxations on cross-ownership of terrestrial, cable, and satellite TV interests, subject to a limit of 15 per cent of the total TV audience, and a loosening of the rules on radio ownership.

For the future the Government has not accepted the argument that regulation will wither away. Although there is clearly some truth in the proposition that in many areas looser regulation will be desirable, this does not mean that the public interest can be reduced entirely to establishing a clear set of rules within which all participants can do what they like. There are four areas where governments, either on a national or, increasingly, an international level, have a legitimate role to play.

Universal access

The first of these is to ensure the opportunity of universal access in the home to the basic services needed for full participation in a democratic society. The almost universal availability and penetration of terrestrial TV allows an enormous range of entertainment, education and information to reach the home for the cost of the licence fee (ignoring the complexities of the imputed costs of advertising-funded channels). It is inevitable that as the market fragments, not only will the range of choice be increased, but that levels of choice will be available on an incremental basis, according to ability and willingness to pay.

There is nothing wrong with this. Indeed millions already enjoy the extra choice. The financial implications of the new competition, though, are enormous. They could lead to the destruction of the traditional, universally available and relatively cheap networks. This would not matter if the new channels were providing the same range of services, however fragmented, at a price everyone could afford. There is no commercial reason for them to do so, and so they should not be expected do this.

Even if channels supported largely by subscription (which is the main income source for new satellite and cable channels) could be afforded by 80% of the population, the effect of damaging the universally available channels with public service obligations would be harmful. It is the poor, and (an increasingly different group) the elderly who are most likely to depend on universally available public service broadcasters for access to well-informed news, top sport, drama at all brow-levels, the arts and science. It would be perverse if the increased availability of new services led, because of the dismantling of the old broadcasting networks, to fewer services being available to the most disadvantaged in society.

As a result of this, Governments should remember that, when they are devising ways to maximise the impact of new convergent communications technologies, they should not neglect the important services provided by traditional means, and should be alive to the need to preserve a basic tier of universally available services. What should be included on such services is itself open to debate, but the best starting-point is the range of positive obligations imposed on the BBC and (to a lesser extent) ITV at present.

Wide distribution of multimedia services

The second obligation on Government is to ensure as wide as possible a distribution of multimedia services. The over-riding need, which the Government has already fulfilled, is to provide a competitive market for the building of networks to the home. Allowing cable TV companies to compete in telephony, while restricting BT's ability to carry entertainment services for a number of years has, after many years of false starts, persuaded the cable industry to start serious building programmes. The long-term need is to ensure that more than one body (in practice, someone as well as BT) has the incentive to provide the potential for broadband services. Just as competition has revolutionised the UK telephony market within a decade, so the provision of digital services will be best served by maintaining a competitive market, rather than blessing an approved leading player.

Under the general heading of provision of multimedia services, the Government will need to consider two related issues. How best to ensure that public buildings are wired up to receive and disseminate these services for those who cannot receive them in the home, and whether to encourage any particular range of content to be carried on such services. The first, especially the provision of services to schools, can best be done on the principle of 'planning gain', and some cable companies have already agreed to this.

The second is an area that has not received much public attention, and deserves some consideration. As some of the time previously spent viewing TV is used with new media products, some of them interactive, it will be a matter of public interest whether a good range of products is available, especially in the educational field. There should be an opportunity here to use existing systems for subsidising broadcasting more flexibly.

The BBC has to meet certain criteria in return for its licence fee income. It is also being increasingly encouraged to develop commercial services. There is clearly a market for educational products, such as CD-ROMs, which the commercial side of the BBC is in an ideal position to meet. For the time being this would not be an activity suitable for funding from the licence fee, which is designed for universal services.

In the future, though, it would be reasonable for the BBC to be asked to produce CD-ROMs, and possibly on-line services, which fulfil its role in education, science arts, natural history and 'civics', either wholly or partly out of licence fee money. These services, even if they were not universally available, could become part of the BBC's core activities in a multimedia world. The funding arrangements for the BBC are due to be reviewed in 2001. This timescale is ideal for considering the ways of funding new on-line services.

Preserving competition

The third legitimate area for Government action is to ensure that the industry remains properly competitive. Technological breakthroughs can often lead to one company obtaining the ability to restrict access to viewers, even if normal commercial activity gained the initial advantage. The biggest immediate issue is dealt with below, in the discussion on gateway monopolies.

The underlying point is the need to maintain fair access to viewers for all broadcasters. Programme makers need a channel to broadcast their efforts. That channel needs a distribution system, whether terrestrial, cable, or satellite. For all pay channels, there needs to be another stage in the journey, when the signal is encrypted, and is then put through a set-top box which unscrambles the signal, and only allows those subscribers who have paid for the service, to receive it. This last 'gateway' function, which comprises control of the encryption technology and the associated subscriber management system, can be a means of choking off competition, if the gateway owner is also a programme maker and distributor.

The media cannot be treated as just another industry

The fourth point for Governments to accept is that the media industry will not be just another industry, even after digital technology has eliminated much of the problem of bandwidth restrictions. It has a unique position in reflecting and transmitting the values of society. The recent White Paper on Media Ownership stated the position well:

> General competition legislation is mainly concerned with securing economic objectives ... However, wider objectives are important so far as the media are concerned. A free and diverse media are an indispensable part of the democratic process. They provide the multiplicity of voices and opinions that informs the public, influences opinion, and engenders political debate. They promote the culture of dissent which any healthy democracy must have. In so doing, they contribute to the cultural fabric of the nation and help define our sense of identity and purpose. If one voice becomes too powerful, this process is placed in jeopardy and democracy is damaged. Special media ownership

rules, which exist in all major media markets, are needed therefore to provide the safeguards necessary to maintain diversity and plurality.[1]

This proposition will still be true in the digital age. Even though the monopoly power endowed by access to scarce bandwidth will disappear, it is already clear that other potential monopolistic powers may emerge without vigilant regulation. So the special dangers of allowing over-powerful media players to emerge will still be there, and Governments cannot withdraw behind general competition laws.

III The immediate regulatory problems

Anti-competitive practices

An issue that needs to be addressed urgently, before any system of digital TV is established, is the problem of gateway monopolies. Even in the current analogue era, this has proved difficult to resolve. Across Europe there are two dominant conditional access systems, which allow broadcasters to sell encrypted channels paid for by subscription. These are owned by BSkyB and Canal Plus, and other broadcasters have been demanding that the control this gives the gatekeepers to set price levels, control the programming intentions of their rivals (since both operators are also programme-makers), and if necessary simply refuse access to viewers, must not be repeated in the digital era.

In July the European Council of Ministers adopted a new Directive on television transmission standards, which did attempt to deal with this problem. The Council agreed that cable or satellite operators who control digital systems should offer access to all broadcasters on 'equitable, reasonable, and non-discriminatory conditions'. It also said that all gatekeepers should keep separate accounts for their activities as conditional access providers.

On the surface, this provides a sensible route forward. Those companies that have had the commercial and technical nous to develop conditional access systems can reap their just rewards, while others are protected. However, regulation after the fact is always likely to be weak. Presumably it would be up to an aggrieved competitor to complain that it is being unfairly treated by a monopoly gatekeeper, and this would enmesh both parties in a legal battle. The alternative, to strike a commercial deal with the gatekeeper, will in practice always be a powerful attraction. In this context, it is instructive to consider the deal BSkyB struck with the two biggest cable operators in the UK, Nynex and Telewest, by which they agreed not to develop rival pay-per-view channels in return for cheap supply of BSkyB channels. With this deal, BSkyB has killed off the possibility of strong rival programming emerging from the UK cable industry. The UK competition authorities initially judged that the agreements were anti-competitive, but whatever their decision, since they cannot force Nynex and Telewest to agree to develop rival services, competition is unlikely to emerge.

In the White Paper on Digital Terrestrial Broadcasting, the Government addresses the issue for this particular type of digital transmission. It says any provider of encryption or subscription management should not discriminate in

---

1. *Media Ownership: The Government's Proposals* CM 2872 (HMSO), paragraph 1.4.

favour of or against any particular multiplex provider or broadcaster, and should not unreasonably refuse to offer its services on fair and reasonable terms. There will be a licensing regime to enforce this, run by OFTEL in conjunction with the Independent Television Commission.

OFTEL will need to be extremely vigilant to ensure that it is not simply reactive under this regime. Equally important is the question of whether the same conditions should be applied to satellite and cable gatekeepers. Since any sensible broadcasting policy in an era of technological convergence should aim to be technology-neutral, there is a good case for creating all-embracing gateway rules, in response to the EC Directive. The ideal long-term solution is genuine competition between gateways, so that viewers can decide which programmes to buy, rather than being forced to accept what the dominant technology is providing.

Some types of programming need universal access

Another problem that is already apparent and which will merely become more acute in the digital era is the preservation of universal access for certain types of programming. The early stage of this necessary balancing act has been seen in the development of ITV, since the 1990 Broadcasting Act removed some of the positive duties on the ITV contractors, but still left them with public service obligations. Inevitably some franchise-holders have wanted to explore the bounds of where their obligations now rest, and the ITC has had to be firm in preserving, for example, a full-length news bulletin in prime time.

The fights over sports rights have been the most dramatic example of how programmes that were once universally available can disappear from screens. So far, none of the biggest national events (the 'Protected List' such as the Cup Final) has signed to a subscription channel, because the audiences on these channels are still relatively small. As audiences and subscription income rise, these channels will become more powerful relative to the advertising-funded or BBC channels, and those sports that have stayed on terrestrial TV because of its universal reach will find it increasingly difficult to resist the large sums on offer. This money has already had beneficial side-effects such as the rebuilding of many top football grounds.

The general lesson to draw from all this is that there needs to be a clear public policy on which types of programming need to be universally available. In addition, whatever list of programmes is agreed, the means of making them universally available needs to be as cost-effective and easy as possible. For at least the next five years, this suggests a continuation of the BBC licence fee. Beyond that, the method of public funding will need to be re-assessed, but it is conceivable that the licence fee will survive.

One of the most powerful reasons for having a mass broadcaster funded non-commercially is the need for independent news and comment on business affairs. With relaxation of cross-media restrictions inevitably leading to tie-ups between newspaper groups, TV companies, and possibly telecommunications interests, it is vital that coverage of the media industry itself is full and fair, as it becomes an ever-more important part of the national economy. It is reasonable, to put it mildly, to be sceptical about the ability of any media outlet to cover its own proprietor's affairs sensibly. This applies to the BBC as much as any commercial broadcaster. At least the existence of the BBC means that news stories about the communications sector cannot come only from the parent companies of the relevant journalists, or their nearest commercial rivals.

IV Potential new problems in the digital age

Clearly the extra choice provided by digital communications will not simply allow Governments to withdraw from media regulation. So it will be important to identify the main areas that digital-era regulation will have to treat.

Maintaining a common culture

The underlying purpose must be to maintain high-quality universal services, which could disappear if the funding base is largely transferred to new, specialist services. This purpose is based on the argument that it is worth preserving a common culture on a national basis. Enthusiasts for cyberspace argue that world-wide communities of common interest will replace the geographically limited loyalties of the past. If they do, so be it: the digital revolution really will be the most important event since the discovery of fire. One is entitled to be sceptical at this stage. Until it happens, it would be short-sighted to allow any diminution in the powers of the existing mass media to bring communities together, to provide shared experiences, and to give citizens the chance to seize the choices and opportunities that are available.

This thought is a special example of an old idea, that the more information a country makes available to all its citizens, the better. Adam Smith favoured universal state-provided education for the express purpose of allowing those in all ranks of society to be able to make sensible judgements about the great issues of the day. In *The Wealth of Nations* he wrote:

> An instructed and intelligent people ... are always more decent and orderly than an ignorant and stupid one. They are more disposed to examine, and more capable of seeing through, the interested complaints of faction and sedition, and they are, upon that account, less apt to be misled into any wanton or unnecessary opposition to the measures of government. In free countries, where the safety of government depends very much upon the favourable judgement which the people may form of its conduct, it must surely be of the highest importance that they should not be disposed to judge rashly or capriciously concerning it.[2]

In a rather faster-moving world, though one no less full of faction or sedition, and probably more disposed to rash and capricious judgements, the provision of relatively fair information to the whole of society is still a noble purpose. (Enthusiasts for public service broadcasting of a right-wing disposition, who may sometimes have felt they were becoming unfashionable, can find great solace in Adam Smith. He was also a keen supporter of the state encouraging those who sought 'to amuse and divert the people by painting, poetry, music, dancing; (and) by all sorts of dramatic representations and exhibitions'.[3])

---

2. Adam Smith *The Wealth of Nations*. (New York: Random House, 1994), p. 846.
3. Adam Smith *The Wealth of Nations*, p. 855.

The full range of services which Governments may wish to see universally available would include independent news, informative children's programmes, science, arts and natural history programmes, local and regional programming, and programmes catering for minorities who would not otherwise be served.

Many of these services would of course be provided by commercial operators. It is likely that the expense of producing them would only be sustainable by a premium subscription service. (The more overtly commercial ITV Network, which can see its advertising growth under threat, is concentrating its fire on a smaller range of top-class programmes.) So Government will have to find some way of making them universally available, whether through traditional means such as the licence fee, or by subsidising access for poorer viewers. The thought occurs that, faced with the prospect of a means-tested licence fee, Governments may remain attached to the current flat-rate poll tax for TV viewers.

Gateways

Another imperative for digital era regulation will be to avoid gateway monopolies, as explained above. If the current vertical integration obtained by programme producers who have also gained a stranglehold on the transponders of the Astra satellite, *and* a decisive lead in subscriber management systems, is allowed to continue unchecked, then the existence of hundreds of channels will be irrelevant. There will be fewer providers with effective access to viewers than in the heavily regulated traditional broadcasting world. Not only would this threaten diversity of opinion, it would also lead to desirable TV offerings, such as sport, being completely run by, and for the benefit of, a small number of TV networks. The sports themselves can only negotiate a decent deal if there is genuinely competitive bidding.

Preserving a national media industry

Government may also wish to preserve a national production base. There is no particular industrial argument for this, since if a country cannot support a particular industry there is no reason for Government fiat to maintain it artificially. Nevertheless, in the cultural field, especially in the dissemination of news and comment, it would be dangerous to rely entirely on acceptable foreign content. Quotas restricting foreign imports are a second-best solution ignoring the wishes of consumers. It is far better to maintain an indigenous industry that can produce material which viewers are eager to see, and which has the capacity to produce the full range of programmes.

Competition between networks

The last imperative will be to preserve competition among the delivery networks. The danger of convergence is that alliances of carriers (whether telecom companies or cable operators), programme makers and subscription management companies, will form an unbreakable vertically integrated chain which will stifle competition. The best long-term way to prevent this is to ensure that there is more than one way for a programme maker to gain access to viewers. Satellite, cable, and terrestrial networks will all have a role to play in a well-regulated digital world.

V Appropriate regulation in the digital era

With all of these pressures in mind, the UK Government will need to recognise three different purposes of regulation in the digital era.

The role of public service broadcasting

The first will be to maintain positive encouragement of universally available public service broadcasting, which would aim to fulfil the following criteria:

- To reflect and promote British culture
- To provide independent news and current affairs programmes
- To make available to the mass of the population important national events
- To expand the interests of audiences, especially in the arts and sciences
- To provide educational programmes for all ages
- To provide worthwhile programmes for children
- To aim at the highest standards of decency

For the time being, this argues for the continuation of the BBC in something recognisably like its current form. While it is possible to devise other blueprints for achieving these objectives, and rather easy to point out where the BBC falls short of them, there is a practical, Tory argument for leaving in place an existing institution that serves a public purpose. The BBC will need to adapt rapidly to the new era, to become faster-moving and more commercial. But it is not obsolete.

Preventing concentration of influence

The second purpose of regulation will be to prevent undue concentration of influence at any stage of the process of conveying material to viewers. Choice will not be enhanced, despite the proliferation of channels, if monopolies develop with the power to restrict new entrants, or to dictate commercial terms to programme-makers, through cross-subsidy or predatory pricing.

In the White Paper on cross-media ownership, the Government opened the debate on how to measure an operator's share of the total media market, on the assumption that convergence would make the control of dominant players in individual media sectors increasingly irrelevant. The key question in this debate is whether an 'exchange rate' between media sectors should be based on audience share or revenues. In other words, how can you calculate the relevant measure that equates a percentage share of the newspaper market with the TV or radio market.

Much of the media industry prefers a measure based on audience share, whether this be newspaper circulation or TV audience share. This is inherently imperfect, for a number of reasons. Firstly, it is not clear that sheer audience size will be a genuine proxy for influence in a subscription-dominated TV world. The more people pay for the most desirable programmes by subscription, the easier it is to assign a value to the intensity of desire of the audience to watch a particular programme or channel, and hence its likely influence over the audience.

There is a separate issue relating to the degree of constraint on the output of a particular medium. Newspapers can say what they like. TV and radio stations have to maintain balance of various viewpoints. So it is inherently more likely that newspapers will influence their readers' views than TV news broadcasts, even though TV is a more powerful medium. Measuring influence is itself hugely difficult. Measuring the relative influence of different media operating under different controls is bound to be arbitrary.

Perhaps most crucially, as new opinion-formers come on stream through the Internet, it will become increasingly difficult to measure their 'audience'. While it is possible to calculate the number of 'hits' on an individual Web site or bulletin board, to expect a regulator to be told how long each hit lasted, or what percentage of them came from outside the UK, will be unwieldy and intrusive. As time passes and technology develops, cross-media measurement based on audience share will become increasingly unrealistic.

So revenue share is overwhelmingly likely to be a more objective measure for a media 'exchange rate'. It is information which is collected and analysed anyway. It reflects both the size of the audience and its level of interest, and it has the same units of account for every medium.

Content regulation

The third purpose of regulation will be in many ways the most difficult. This will be to maintain controls over unacceptable content, whether it be pornographic, violent, or terrorist-inspired. Already the international nature of the Internet has shown that on-line services which run worldwide can offend hugely at the receiving end, while being legal at the point of origin. To a lesser degree, satellite TV throws up the same problems but so far the relatively public nature of any TV channel has made it practical to regulate unacceptable content on a national basis.

Assuming that it will be impossible to agree a world-wide code for content on the Internet, given the different mores in different continents, the best hope seems to be filtering technology, which will allow each home to determine what types of on-line service can be allowed entry. The role of public regulators may be to approve different systems, so that non-technically-minded customers can at least have some confidence in the filter.

VI Conclusions

Regrettably, there is no guarantee that the immense power to communicate given to societies and individuals by the digital revolution will lead to greater plurality of expression, or greater ease of entrance into the home for new voices. The need for Governments to legislate and regulate to protect pluralism will remain. The biggest change will be that increasing amounts of this regulation will have to take place at an international level, if it is to be effective.

So far, the measured tread taken by the UK Government towards deregulation is sensible. The ability to measure a total media market will never be perfect, and will need to based on objective criteria. Revenue looks the most promising. Whatever measuring system emerges, there will still need to be a positive commitment to continuing public service broadcasting, enabling widespread access to high-quality material across the range of traditional and new media. There must also be an unwavering opposition to the development of monopolies in the communications sector.

The opportunity for a digital age to provide entertainment, information and education to millions of people in a way that allows them greater control over their lives would have intrigued a liberal thinker like Adam Smith. It should not be allowed to sink into the dystopian vision of a more contemporary thinker, Bruce Springsteen, with his nightmare of '57 channels and nothing on'.

The South East Essex
College of Arts & Technology

Exchange Rates and Gatekeepers

Andrew Graham*

I Introduction

In May 1995 the Government published a White Paper containing proposals for reforming the regulation of the media.[1] In this they stated that they would legislate at the earliest possible opportunity to relax many present restrictions on cross-ownership of the media and that in the longer term there would be further reform based on a system that would 'define the total media market'. They also announced that they would like to encourage debate on the longer term proposals and requested comments by 31 August 1995. Shortly before this deadline two other relevant documents have appeared. On 8 August OFTEL published a major consultative document, *Beyond the Telephone, the Television and the PC*[2] and on 10 August the Government published *Digital Terrestrial Broadcasting: The Government's Proposals*.[3] (In what follows the publication on Media Ownership is referred to as 'the White Paper'. Other publications are referenced in the usual way.)

This paper is a contribution to the debate. First, it takes issue with one of the Government's core longer term propositions. The Government suggests in the White Paper that the media should be viewed as a single market and that there should be an 'exchange rate [between different media sectors] based on objective measurable factors' (para 6.13). The belief that technical change is causing previously separate media to overlap is well based, but the proposal that there should be an 'exchange rate' based on 'objective' factors is seriously flawed. This is discussed in Section II.

Second, this paper argues that there are critical questions about 'gatekeepers' that are not adequately dealt with in the Government's proposals. Control of these access points to the Information Superhighway, in particular control of the set-top boxes for televisions, may prove to be far more important than direct market dominance both in determining access *now* and, more important, in having a critical influence on the *future shape* of the media industry. It follows that the distinction in the Government's proposals between the short term and the long term therefore breaks down. Most important, it will be shown below that a failure to act *now* to

*I would like to thank Howard Smith and Peggotty Graham for helpful comments on a first draft of this paper. I am also grateful to members of the IPPR Media Advisory Group for useful discussion of some of the issues raised here. As usual, responsibility for any errors remains my own.

1. Cm 2872. *Media Ownership: the Government's Proposals* (London HMSO) 1995.

2. OFTEL. *Beyond the Telephone, The Television and the PC: Consultative Document* (London OFTEL) August 1995.

3. Cm 2946. *Digital Terrestrial Broadcasting: The Government's Proposals* (London HMSO) 1995.

ensure common standards is likely to create a situation in which some consumers, unwilling to buy a multiplicity of set-top boxes, would be dependent on only a single supplier for all their news, information and entertainment. In other words *individual consumers could well face an undesirable concentration of media influence even when no such concentration would be apparent at the level of the industry as a whole*. These arguments are set out in Section III. Alternative proposals are in Section IV.

II The media – economic and political concerns

Concern about dominance of the media arises from two different considerations – the economic and the political. The Government recognises this distinction in the White Paper. However, regrettably, the policy conclusions that are drawn do not take this fully on board.

Economic concerns

The *economic* concern about dominance in the media industry is the desire to avoid monopoly power. In this respect the media is no different from any other good. The worry is that if a single firm controls too much of the market excessive prices will be charged. In the media these prices include both the prices charged to the consumer and the prices charged to other firms for the provision of advertising. Moreover, in this case there are, at least in principle, objective measures of what is meant by 'the market' and of the adverse effects of concentration. Goods are in the same market if the price elasticity of one good with respect to the other is high (in the limiting case goods are identical to one another when the relevant price elasticity is infinite). Similarly the adverse effects, if any, of concentration can be measured (at least in principle) by the price increase following from a merger.

There are, of course, several well-known complications. On the one hand firms may adopt a variety of uncompetitive practices as an alternative to, or in addition to, charging monopoly prices. For example, in the computer industry these include low price introductory offers which can 'lock' customers into particular systems only for them to face higher prices for compatible hardware or software later, or agreements from one sector to another that would pass unnoticed in simple measures of competition or concentration. On the other hand firms may be restrained from charging excessive prices by potential competition as well as by actual competition. In addition, such issues become more complicated where there is technical change. Here, a degree of monopoly can even be in the public interest since the search for monopoly profits can be one factor driving the technology forward and, if technical change is rapid, no public policy intervention may be required – the process of change may itself be a sufficient discipline on the monopolist. This is especially likely if the sources of technical change are diffuse. Nonetheless how much market dominance is justified and for how long remains an issue and is difficult to judge.

However, such complications apply to all markets. Moreover, these issues, problematic as they may be in practice, are exactly those dealt with by normal competition law and by the relevant regulatory authorities (in the UK the Monopolies and Mergers Commission and the Director General of Fair Trading). These are also matters with which other regulators, such as OFTEL, are rapidly becoming involved. Thus, though the speed of technical change in the media undoubtedly adds to the complexity of the situation, there is nothing new *in principle* about this problem. Technical change is always altering the boundaries of one industry compared with another. There is therefore no case on these grounds to alter the regulatory framework.

It follows that there is also no case on *economic* grounds to establish 'exchange rates' between one media sector and another. On the contrary if the Government were to legislate to this effect, they would be prejudging work that is elsewhere left to the empirical investigations of the Office of Fair Trading or the Monopolies and Mergers Commission. There would therefore be a potential conflict between one part of the law and another.

Political concerns

The reason, of course, that the Government proposes special treatment for the media is that there are also a set of political concerns. As the White Paper states:

> Television, radio and the press have a unique role in the free expression of ideas and opinion, and thus in the democratic process. The main objective must therefore be to secure a plurality of sources of information and opinion, and a plurality of editorial control over them. (para 5.2); and

> United Kingdom general competition law is concerned primarily with the operation of economic markets rather than with the distinctive wider needs of public policy in relation to the media industry: in particular the need to ensure the expression of a rich diversity of views and opinions. (para 5.8)

It is equally true, as the Government claims, that technical change is causing the collapse of the previous segmentation of the media market and that a new legislative framework is required to reflect this change. What does *not* follow from this is the claim in the White Paper that there should be an 'exchange rate based on objective measurable factors' (para 6.12) so that the different media sectors can be regulated as a total media market.

The fundamental problem with this proposition is that, in the political sphere, there are no such objectively measurable factors that can be used to combine the different parts of the media. The fallacy in assuming that there might be such objective factors can be seen from two different standpoints. First, the *variety* of measures is itself a problem. Second, there is the more fundamental question of whether, in principle, *any* measure could ever be objective when the ultimate concern must be the *political* question: which is what form of media industry is consistent with a democratic society?

The variety of measures

Possible measures suggested for establishing exchange rates between different parts of the media include (a) advertising revenue, (b) total revenue (advertising plus subscription and sales), (c) circulation and/or audience, and (d) time. There are, at least, the following three reasons why none of these measures could be used to establish 'objective' exchange rates:

(i) They give radically different results. For example, radio generates relatively little revenue, but is listened to for many hours. It would therefore appear small on one measure, but large on another. Which is the 'objective' result?

(ii) Particular results are favoured by particular groups. For example, News International[4] supports what it calls 'influence' as the objective factor. In practice they measure this using time. In contrast, the British Media Industry Group,[5] representing Associated Newspapers (the *Daily Mail*), Pearsons (the *Financial Times*), the *Guardian* and the *Telegraph* favour what it calls 'share of voice', but which is in fact audience/circulation. The results are sharply different. The first makes News International look relatively small, the second does the same for the British Media Industry Group. One can be forgiven for observing that such results coincide with the interests of each of the groups that have suggested them. Moreover, both News International and the British Media Industry Group include public service broadcasters in their measures. This has the effect of making *both* groups look much smaller than would otherwise be the case and of making the BBC appear particularly large.

(iii) All these measures are highly dependent on a range of questionable and/or arbitrary assumptions. Measures based on revenue, for example, face the obvious objection that some television is financed by a licence fee, some by advertising and some by subscription. How are these to be combined? Moreover, any revenue based measure necessarily gives higher weight to the media consumption of the rich than the poor – hardly the right approach in a democratic society. And, with measures based on time, who is to say whether an hour listening to radio is the same as an hour reading a newspaper or an hour watching television? Similar objections exist to any measure based on audience or circulation.

The *variety* of possible measures combined with different results, special pleading and arbitrary assumptions make it highly unlikely that any search for a single 'objective' measure will succeed. However, it might still be thought that the arguments above are matters of detail, which could eventually be resolved by further research. Such a conclusion would be a mistake.

To see why this is so it is necessary to return to first principles. The fundamental point about the role of the media in a democratic society is that it has become the central place in which ideas are exchanged, debated and created. It is, as I have remarked elsewhere, the 'prime way through which ideas, common-sense beliefs and issues of the day emerge and become shared knowledge in a nearly nationwide audience ... [such ideas] are also 'common knowledge', that is, not only does everyone know them, but everyone knows that everyone knows them. This is not

---

4. Shew, W.B. 'UK Media Concentration' A Report prepared for News International plc, July 1994.

5. British Media Industry Group. *A New Approach to Cross Media Ownership* (London British Media Industry Group) 21 March 1995.

only a precondition for the solution of many coordination problems in society, but also enhances the rational collective debate that democracy should be about'.[6]

Once this point is sharply in focus, it is clear that neither diversity of view nor plurality of ownership, nor even diversity of editorial viewpoint are *sufficient* conditions for the media in a democratic society. Multiple owners and multiple editors publishing a wide variety of views, but all of which were of doubtful validity and/or were factually inaccurate would be permitted by such conditions, but such a situation would hardly be desirable. Conversely, if a large share of the market were held by an editor of integrity totally committed to impartiality, truth and freedom of expression, this would be perfectly acceptable from a democratic point of view.

The same point can be made by reconsidering the suggestion made by News International that what matters about media power is 'influence' and that this can best be measured by the time devoted to a particular media supplier. What this implies is that the more the time spent on a particular supplier the greater the *undue* influence it has. However, this ignores *the sources of the influence or the purposes of the supplier*. If this position were to be taken seriously a far bigger threat to a democratic society would come from school where people spend years at a time with a single supplier, than from any dominance of the media. The reason this is rarely suggested is that the *purpose* of a school is not to indoctrinate, but to educate. Indeed the exception proves the rule. In the rare number of cases when people do object to the influence of schools it is usually because the school is suspected of peddling a particular point of view to the detriment of education.

The central point being made here is that there is no way of using the same scale to measure different editorial *purposes*. The idea of giving a certain 'weight' to left wing media or to right wing media or to impartial media is simply misconceived. This is true *even within the same media*. A television programme on a religious channel maintaining that the world was created in seven days, cannot be placed on the same footing as a balanced programme about the strengths and weaknesses of Darwinian theory. The same is true *a fortiori* as between different media. In the *political* domain, there cannot therefore be an 'objective' measurable way of combining different media players. To try to do so is to commit what philosophers describe as a category error. In plain English, it is to try to mix chalk with cheese.

To some extent the *existing* regulatory framework recognises this distinction through public service obligations and through the separate Charter for the BBC. What ought to be done is to build on this distinction. How this might be achieved is discussed further in Section III below.

III Gatekeepers to the highway

A second aspect of the Government's proposals that gives grounds for serious concern is the role of 'gatekeepers' to the new media. 'Gatekeepers' arise wherever there are bottlenecks through which information has to pass and where the passage

---

6. Graham, A. 'Public Policy and the Information Superhighway: the scope for strategic intervention, co-ordination and top-slicing' in R.Collins and J. Purnell (eds.) *Managing the Information Society*, p. 40. (London, Institute for Public Policy Research, 1995).

through such bottlenecks can be controlled. Leaving the Internet on one side, there is currently only one such gateway – the set-top box that controls access to Sky Television. But there will shortly be more. Under the proposals just announced by the Government about digital terrestrial broadcasting (Cm 2946) set-top boxes will soon be required to receive channels broadcast terrestrially but in a digital form. Digital terrestrial broadcasting will also require what are termed 'multiplexers'. These are operators who will combine several programmes (plus other services) into a single channel for broadcasting. Once licences have been allocated to multiplexers they will control who sends what bits of digital information. These also could therefore become an important gateway.

So far it is the first of these (the so-called 'conditional access arrangements') which has generated most discussion. The White Paper reports that the earlier consultation carried out by the Government found that this was a key issue 'which needed to be addressed' (para 4.9). The White Paper also states that 'the future regulation of media ownership will critically depend upon the proper operation of the market for broadcasting services, including the subscription systems through which pay television services control revenue and customer information' (para 5.12). Yet the Government says nothing more beyond the fact that these conditional access arrangements will be subject to normal competition law both in the UK and in the European Community.

This is unsatisfactory on four counts: the present position of satellite broadcasting and BSkyB where a small monopoly may develop into a larger one, the effect of this on digital broadcasting, the confusion that exists over UK and EU law and the adverse effects of this confusion on common standards, and the inadequacy of competition law as a means of dealing with conditional access arrangements. Each of these points is developed further below.

Satellite broadcasting and the present position of BSkyB

At present there are several satellites that beam channels to Europe, such as Eutelsat and Intelsat, but nearly all of the English language broadcasts available in the UK come from the Astra satellites, 1a, 1b, 1c and 1d.[7] The channels available from these are heavily dominated by Sky Television (owned by BSkyB which is, in turn, 50 per cent owned by News International).[8] Further, access to the great majority of the channels available from Sky are dependent on the payment (by monthly direct debit) of a subscription. It is this subscription plus the set-top box and a card inserted into the box that allows access to programmes broadcast in an encrypted form. At the moment these are the only set-top boxes marketed in the UK. News International therefore has a monopoly of them, a monopoly derived in turn from its monopoly of satellite broadcasting.

This monopoly is not, in itself, particularly serious as satellite broadcasting is still such a small part of total broadcasting (less than 8 per cent by time). However, there is already concern about the extent to which access to some viewing of sport

---

7. 1a, 1b and 1c are exclusively analogue. 1d is analogue but has digital capacity. Three further digital satellites will be launched soon – 1e in October 1995, 1f in early 1996, and 1g in mid-1997.

8. According to the Financial Times' *New Media Markets* BSkyB's share of Astra was approximately 60 per cent in the first half of 1995.

is dominated by BSkyB. In addition, a recent agreement between BSkyB and the cable companies, TeleWest and Nynex Cablecomms Ltd is a good illustration of the extent to which simple measures of concentration fail to capture the complexity of anti-competitive practices.[9]

The implications for digital broadcasting

Second, and far more important, is the implication of BSkyB's present monopoly for digital broadcasting – the next stage in the development of broadcasting. Digital broadcasting can be either terrestrial or satellite, but both will require set-top boxes (all TV sets are currently analogue so a box to convert digital to analogue will be needed, at least until TV sets become digital). Without an insistence on common standards these set-top boxes are unlikely to be fully compatible. Currently there is no such insistence. There is thus the danger that one or other of the following will occur. Either there will be one set-top box (BSkyB's) with everyone needing access to this or there will be several potentially incompatible set-top boxes. Either of these outcomes would be socially undesirable and/or economically inefficient.

The single set-top box outcome is undesirable on both economic and political grounds because of the potential monopoly that this hands to BSkyB. Moreover, this will not be easily solved by regulation. There will be at least two kinds of problems as the result of such a monopoly. One will concern the attribution of costs – any regulator is unlikely to be able to check for certain that fair prices are being charged. The other concerns the design of modern computer systems. These are typically based on menus of choices (or, as systems become more sophisticated, on 'browsers' or 'navigation systems'). If control of these rests with BSkyB, or indeed with any single supplier, it will be relatively easy to skew consumers' choices by the order in which programmes are presented on the screen or by the criteria available for browsing or navigating.

A situation of several incompatible set-top boxes is undesirable both socially and economically. Currently the boxes cost £300-400. Consumers will therefore face either higher costs (if they buy more than one set-top box) or reduced choice (if they do not). Since many consumers will choose only to buy a single box (or even none at all since no single box will give access to the full range of programmes), manufacturers and programme makers will face smaller markets and higher unit costs. There is a real danger in this case that the UK will become stuck in what economists describe as 'a low level equilibrium' – small and unnecessarily fragmented markets will reduce choice, raise costs, lower demand and reduce investment.

Such fragmentation needs to be avoided on social, cultural and democratic grounds as much as because of the economic costs. At present the UK can take pride

---

9. These cable companies were offered discounts if they bought bundles of Sky programmes and, in return for this, Sky programmes were to receive priority allocation on the cable channels. In addition these cable companies agreed not to carry services which might hurt services provided by Sky. Following investigation by the OFT the discounts were reduced and offered to other cable companies but, at the time of writing, the remainder of the agreement was still being considered by the OFT on the grounds that it was thought to be 'significantly anti-competitive'.
Office of Fair Trading. 'OFT Studies BSkyB Proposals' Press Release 20 July 1995;
Office of Fair Trading. 'OFT approves amended BSkyB rate card for cable industry' Press Release 18 August 1995.

in high quality television. At the core of this system is public service broadcasting that is *universally* available. If the way in which digital television is introduced causes fragmentation, irreversible damage will be done. Socially, 'the viewing of television is part of what creates a sense of commonality'[10] and with greater fragmentation there will be less commonality. Culturally, national events such as the VJ day commemorations or the Cup Final should be available to all, rather than dependent on ownership of a particular set-top box. Democratically, it would be quite wrong if particular consumers relied for their information, education and entertainment on the possibly narrow views of a single supplier of television, rather than being exposed to a plurality of views.

In the light of these factors it is extraordinary that the Government's proposals on Media Ownership are presented as if digital television is an afterthought and as if common standards for set-top boxes are an optional extra rather than the *key* to the future *competitive and democratic* development of the industry.

UK and European law and common standards

The obvious solution to this problem would be to make common standards manda-tory for conditional access systems. This was proposed by the European Parliament in 1994, but was strongly resisted by the UK. As a result in December 1994 the European Council decided that a common interface would be an option, but *not* a requirement, for manufacturers of set-top boxes. Under the new co-decision proce-dures a second round of discussions followed between the Parliament and the Council. A compromise position was reached in the 'Caudron Report'.[11] Two of the key points of this report, adopted at the Council of Ministers of 24 July and incorporated into a European Directive, are (a) that operators of conditional access systems when granting licences to manufacturers shall ensure that this is 'done under fair, reasonable and non-discriminatory terms' and (b) that, in granting licences, they shall not make the licences subject to 'conditions prohibiting, deter-ring or discouraging the inclusion in the same product of a common interface allowing the connection of several access systems'.

This is better than nothing yet the view of the British Government remains, at best, unclear. In their White Paper on Digital Terrestrial Broadcasting they state that 'The Government wishes to avoid a situation in which providers of encryption systems, or of subscription management systems, can favour one broadcaster, or multiplex provider, over another.' They also say that providers of these systems to 'terrestrial' multiplex providers or broadcasters will be licensed under the Telecom-munications Act after consultation on the conditions with the ITC and that 'the licence conditions will reflect the EC Directive'.[12] This is a move in the right direction. However, quite how this 'reflection' will occur remains to be seen. In the immediately following sentence the Government say they 'will be considering further the implementation of this Directive'. More fundamentally, 'satellite' broad-casters are not mentioned. Here obscurity reigns.

---

10. Graham, A and G. Davies. 'The Public Funding of Broadcasting' in T. Congdon *et al.*, *Paying for Broadcasting*, p. 182. (London, Routledge, 1992).

11. European Parliament. The 'Caudron' Report 31 May. DOC EN\RR\275\275109 and PE 212.822/fin, 1995

12. Cm 2946, para 4.17.

One reason for this unsatisfactory position appears to be that the British Government and the European Council seem to have been swayed by fears that mandatory standards would delay investment. The 'simulcrypt' system offered by BSkyB (and by Canal+, Premiere, Filmnet and Telepiu) was very close to being launched. The 'multi-crypt' for the common interface was not. Closely linked has been the view that BSkyB has done the critical investment and deserves its reward. This latter point is fair enough, but there are two weaknesses in the argument.

First, if the conditional access systems are broken down into their constituent parts it can be seen that they are not especially technically complex. Even for the proposed digital transmissions there are just three stages: (a) conversion from digital information to an analogue based video image, (b) the unscrambling of encrypted transmissions and (c) a payment record. The first of these is standard in modern computing (it is little more than a modem in reverse), the second is equally standard and the third is no more than a database plus an electronic card. At the moment Sky includes information in its broadcasts that allows a card to be activated or deactivated depending on whether payments have been made. However, if contact with the viewer were made by telephone and if payment was 'per view', payments could be effected as they are now in Swindon with a Mondex card (or even just with a credit card). In this case there would not even need to be a separate subscription management service. It follows that the cost of conditional access systems does not need to be high and the current costs (some £300-400 per set-top box) could fall rapidly with economies of scale (just as they have with modems). It also seems improbable that systems with a common interface would be long in coming forward.

Second, and more fundamental, the view that common standards would delay investment is putting the cart before the horse. Of course common standards would reduce the return to BSkyB and so might somewhat reduce *their* investment, but this totally overlooks the economics of network industries. A common standard is the factor that will (a) encourage all *other* manufacturers, (b) ensure that the economies of scale from high volume production of *compatible* set-top boxes are captured (once there is common standard one would expect competition and high volume to coexist, whereas without common standards, there will be neither) and (c) facilitate the so-called 'any to any' connections on which network industries depend.

The Government's failure to take adequate account of the last point is particularly surprising. When communications follow an 'any to any' model any maker of a programme or any supplier of a media based service can reach all consumers without let or hindrance. This is essential to competition and the Government has, rightly, espoused such a model in its advocacy of the Information Superhighway, but it seems unwilling to act according to its own avowed goals. Moreover, the importance of this point and the crucial role of common standards in bringing it about ought to be clear from the example of the Internet. Once the common standard of TCP/IP was established, the growth rate of the Internet was explosive. In contrast the Government seems so wedded to the ideology of the 'free market' that it cannot recognise when intervention is required to allow the market to work.

Conditional access – why existing competition law is not enough
The reasons why competition law is insufficient for handling conditional access

arise from arguments made earlier. First, competition law is primarily *negative* being concerned with preventing monopolies or controlling anti-competitive practices. It is not concerned with setting standards nor with the need to intervene *positively* to reap the full benefits of network externalities. A similar point is made by OFTEL who argue (OFTEL, 1995) that none of the Government's proposals about Media Ownership tackle vertical integration. The White Paper focuses almost exclusively on horizontal measures of dominance at the expense of vertical and proposes no changes to competition law. In contrast, OFTEL's provisional conclusion is that 'proactive regulation will be required in respect of dominant Broadband Switchable Mass market distribution systems' (OFTEL, 1995, para 5.2.5).

Second, as has been shown above, there is the importance of conditional access to the future shape of the media. Here especially, competition law is not sufficient. Suppose, for example, that several manufacturers compete to produce set-top boxes and that, because of the competition, there is no monopoly pricing. Suppose further that the channels supplied via these boxes are also at competitive prices. The requirements of competition are thereby satisfied. Yet, if the boxes are incompatible, a major problem remains. Many consumers, reluctant to buy more than one box and facing significant 'switching costs' in moving from one supplier to another, will effectively be dependent upon a single supplier. In other words *individual* consumers might well face an undesirable monopoly of media influence *even when no such concentration was apparent at the level of the industry as a whole.* Moreover, the fact that other channels were available at similar prices and so, in this sense, consumers were offered choice, would not be an adequate defence. In the case of the media it is a requirement of a democratic society that citizens should have *actual* access to a diversity of views and opinions. Potential access is not good enough. But these are not the considerations that are predominant with competition law.

Of course it could be argued that the fragmentation on which this argument depends will not occur. In particular it might be suggested that 'industry standards' will emerge 'naturally' through the pressure on suppliers to collaborate (suppliers can see, as well as anyone else, that consumers will not want a proliferation of set-top boxes). However, it is possible to agree that such pressure will exist, and yet still conclude that public policy should make common standards mandatory. Even with such pressure: (a) there is no guarantee that a single standard will emerge (as the example of IBM PCs and Apple Macs illustrates), (b) even partial fragmentation is sufficient to produce a situation in which individual consumers face monopoly suppliers, (c) if partial fragmentation does occur it could be a costly and lengthy process to reverse and (d) whatever might happen in theory, in practice there are *already* signs of some proliferation of standards.

The fact is that if one takes seriously the requirement that there should be a diversity of media suppliers, then common standards are essential. In this industry, *common standards are the prerequisite for common carriers and common carriers are the prerequisite for media competition and for unhindered access to information.* In other words the right public policy for these critical points in the Information Superhighway may prove to be far more important than direct market dominance both in determining access *now* and in having a critical influence on the *future shape* of the media industry. Moreover, this point is of *immediate* concern and cannot be left to evolve from a longer term debate.

IV Alternative proposals

What then should be done? The most immediate task for the Government is to tackle the problem of the digital gatekeepers. Action is needed now in order both to create the conditions in which digital terrestrial television may flourish and to avoid longer term dominance of the media by proprietorial control of the gateways. In particular it is suggested that the Government has a responsibility to bring about common interfaces and it is not (yet) too late for this to be achieved. There is still the opportunity for the Government to lead. The European Directive has to be enforced. This is the minimum starting point. However, there is no reason the UK should not go beyond this. The way that this should be done is to build on the proposal put forward by the Independent Television Commission on 18 July 1995 that it should draw up a code of practice on conditional access and that conditional access services should be a licensable activity. In particular this code should include common interfaces and these should be made mandatory.

Second, both in the short term and in the longer term it is crucial that a clear distinction should be drawn between concern arising from excessive economic concentration and undue political power. Economic concentration should be dealt with by existing competition law. In particular it should be left to the relevant authorities in that field to judge how far single markets do (or do not) exist by conventional economic criteria and taking account of technical change as it occurs. There is neither a need for nor any case for a media 'exchange rate' to be developed.

None of this means that the Government has been wrong to look afresh at media ownership. Moreover, there is a good case for supposing that a new structure of regulation, looking primarily *across* different media is appropriate (but it should not look exclusively at horizontal issues since, as outlined earlier, anti-competitive activities can also occur vertically). However, this does not mean that all media can now be treated as one market. Nor does it necessarily imply that there should be a *single* regulator (which is what the Government suggests). This looks administratively tidy, but it carries the risk of putting too much power into the hands of one body. In addition, where there are multiple criteria to be borne in mind (as there so obviously are in the case of the media and as the Government recognises) democracy is often better served by having different bodies standing up for different goals. The debate between the goals is then out in the open rather than hidden behind closed doors.

Beyond this the way forward might lie in three directions. First, ownership restrictions should have regard not to any single measure of the total media market, but, instead be based on a series of indicators market by market, with a variety of trigger points based on different combinations of these indicators. This idea has been suggested by James Purnell and Richard Collins.[13]

---

13. Purnell, J. and R.Collins. 'An Evaluation of UK Ownership Rules' (forthcoming, 1995).

Second, instead of the existing structure that, in effect, distinguishes between the public and private sectors with the former carrying public service obligations laid down in the BBC Charter and the latter facing ownership restrictions, there should be a split between the 'guiding principles' under which organisations in all parts of the media wish to participate (John Kay has suggested a similar scheme[14]). Those who wish to trade as 'impartial' should have different rights and obligations from those that clearly represent an interest. In any scheme of this sort those who met the criteria that allowed them to count as 'impartial' would face less scrutiny on grounds of dominance. Indeed, once such a scheme was in operation there would be little reason to include the 'impartial' in any measures of concentration. This would be what the organisation would gain in 'rights'. Conversely, to count as impartial the organisation would have to be far more accountable than now for 'content'. This would be what it would take on in 'obligations'. These rights and obligations would need either to be defined in statute or to be overseen by a statutory body. Such a distinction would tackle head on the *political* dimension to the media discussed above.

Third, there should be at least three bodies looking across the media as a whole. One should be the competition authorities. A second should be a body concerned with matters of taste and decency (and possibly privacy) and a third should be a body dealing with 'the public interest'. The 'public interest' could follow quite closely the lines suggested by the White Paper where it speaks of 'promoting diversity .... expression of a range of views, accuracy in factual information and ... accuracy and impartiality in news provision' (para 6.19). However, there would be three important differences from the proposals made in the White Paper. First, there would be the three bodies, rather than the single regulator suggested by the Government. Second, the public interest regulator would have the power to ask the competition authorities to investigate particular matters relevant to the media such as common standards or the promotion of diversity to *individual* consumers. And third, any organisation in any part of the media, could choose to trade as 'impartial' (whereas the Government restricts its reference to 'accuracy and impartiality in news provision' to the 'broadcast' media). The proposal here is thus that the public interest regulator would look at *all* parts of the media, including new media such as the Internet.

Two final points should be emphasised. First, where media organisations choose not to be accountable as 'impartial' and yet remain small, the role of the public interest regulator would be minimal. Second, the new media *must* be included. Unless they are, not only will the new proposals become rapidly out of date, but the very same distortions set up by the 1990 Broadcasting Act (which excluded non-domestic satellite from the restriction of cross-ownership) will be created afresh.

---

14. Kay, J. (1995) 'News like baked beans better for choice' *Daily Telegraph* 15 May.

Market Share as a Measure of Media Concentration

Bill Robinson*

I Introduction

R apid technological and structural changes in the newspaper, radio and television industries have prompted a reassessment of the framework of media regulation laid down in the Fair Trading Act 1973 and the Broadcasting Act 1990. That is the basic reason for the publication of a paper on media ownership[1] setting out long term proposals for regulation of the industry.

A fundamental aim of the paper, as of the Broadcasting Act which preceded it, is to ensure a plurality of sources of information and opinion, and a plurality of editorial control over them. This *pluralism* is an essential component of modern democracy. In order to protect pluralism, it is proposed to regulate the media by ownership restrictions based on market shares, beyond the normal extent of competition law.

Each of 'the media' is no more than a medium of transmission and we should never forget that the 'product' in this industry is the information, opinion and entertainment that the media deliver. The media command regulatory attention because of the influence conferred by control over the *mass* distribution of the product into millions of homes. This ability to reach huge audiences means the media are credited with the power to swing elections and make fortunes.

The objective of regulation is to prevent any media controller from gaining excessive power in the market for ideas which he can abuse, for instance, by:

- transmitting information which is biased, selective or untrue;

- crossing the borderline separating legitimate expression of opinion from propaganda;

- charging exorbitant prices.

There is a further general objective of media regulation which is the preservation of a national cultural identity. This objective is pursued by the creation and maintenance of a public service broadcaster and by content regulation of the commercial

* The author is deeply indebted to Stephen Banks, Neil Reeder and Jonathan Davis, all colleagues at London Economics, for their substantial contributions to this paper.

1. *Media Ownership: the Government's Proposals*, 1995.

channels, rather than by restrictions on ownership, and is outside the scope of this paper.

In the past regulation in this field has focused more on the means of delivery (the media) than on the products themselves ('the message'). This reflects the fact that, until quite recently, the number of television channels, radio stations, newspapers etc., capable of reaching mass audiences was quite small. In other words it has been in the *distribution* function that there has been the potential for players to achieve dominant positions.

By contrast, the *production* of radio and television programmes and newspaper articles takes place in a reasonably competitive market. There are many small independent television producers, and freelance newspaper and television journalists. Information (news gathering) and entertainment (mainly films) is increasingly dominated by a few large players, but that is not true of opinion. There are many small producers of documentaries and current affairs programmes but not, still, many outlets for them.

The change which has prompted the publication of the White Paper has been a rapid proliferation of methods of distribution. The application of computer technology in the newspaper and magazine industry has reduced costs and led to a massive increase in the number of titles. The arrival of satellite and cable in the television industry has hugely increased choice in the 3.2 million homes with a satellite dish, and the 1 million connected to cable. The video recorder, almost unknown in 1980 and now ubiquitous, has proved of major importance as a new distribution channel for filmed entertainment.

In this paper, we set out to:

- examine more closely what are the key elements of the pluralism that we wish to protect;

- explore the relationship between the market share and the influence of different media companies; and

- consider how regulation of the media market, based on market share, can protect pluralism.

II The meaning of pluralism

Although the Government's paper considers in some detail how to measure market share, it does not discuss the relationship between the definition of the *objective* (pluralism), and the definition of the *instrument* (ownership thresholds based on market share) used to achieve that objective.

In order to decide how to achieve pluralism, the starting point must be to define what the term means. There are a number of dimensions of pluralism: political and commercial *influence*, audience *access* to a range of products and services, and diversity of *content*. This list – not necessarily definitive – helps to clarify the meaning of pluralism, and its relationship with the market share measurement. The aims of a policy for pluralism might include some or all of the following elements:

(1) restricting the political influence of any one firm (e.g. in news, current affairs and the arts);

(2) a balance of political views in media products which have political influence;

(3) restricted influence of any one company in the media at large, e.g. in all audio-visual entertainment or the provision of news;

(4) access to the media for all sectors of society; and

(5) diversity of media product.

Items (1) and (2) are concerned with *political influence*; item (3) with *commercial influence* (i.e. the ability to pursue a particular corporate agenda); item (4) is concerned with *access* to the media; item (5) is concerned with *diversity of content*. These three elements of pluralism -influence, access and content – are clearly very different and need quite different policy measures to help to achieve them.

Successive British governments have created and sustained a public service broadcaster (PSB) and given it a remit to provide diverse programming output and to cater for minorities. We expect the PSB also to maintain balance in its presentation of political views. The remit of the PSB in the UK, therefore, is to help to satisfy aims (1), (2), (4) and (5).

UK broadcasting policy also uses content regulation to maintain the standards expected of the PSB in the private sector. There is, however, one thing that neither a PSB nor content regulation can achieve and that is prevent the emergence of a dominant private sector player in the media that uses its influence to further its corporate agenda and possibly to exert political influence as part of that agenda. It is this aspect of pluralism, captured in aim (3) above, that is being addressed by the White Paper.

Measuring media market concentration

The Department of National Heritage (DNH) approach is based on the traditional division of the media into three sectors: television, radio and newspapers. The proposed thresholds for market share which define the scope of the regulator's discretion are:

- 10% of the UK media market;

- 20% of the media market in any one of either Scotland, Wales, Northern Ireland or each English region;

- 20% of any sectoral (television, press or radio) market.

The crucial issue is how the market shares are to be measured in each sector. There are three options:

- *numbers* of viewers, listeners or readers;

- *time* spent viewing, listening or reading;

- *revenue* from advertising, sponsorship, licence fees, subscriptions and other income sources.

The standard approach in competition policy is to use revenues as the basic measure of market power, and this approach can reasonably be applied in the case of the media. However, given the special concern with influence, there are obvious attractions in using the sheer number of people reached or the number of man-hours spent in consuming media products as the measure of market share. We analyse the attractions and drawbacks of these different options below.

III Regulation and competition in the media

The aim of competition policy

The competitive ideal is that all the firms in any market are charging prices which exactly reflect the costs of production, including a normal return on capital. Firms whose returns are better than this are said to be enjoying monopoly rents. Such rents should, in theory, attract new entrants into the market, bidding down prices and eliminating the rents. But in some industries, including the media, entry is difficult (e.g. because of the huge capital requirements). In such industries regulation has an important role to play in preventing the incumbents from extracting monopoly rents. Regulation of markets to achieve effective competition involves not only the lowest prices but also the highest quality and choice of products and services.

The extraction of monopoly rents is typically easier the greater the market share, which is why competition policy focuses on this measure. This does not mean that companies with large market shares always abuse the power that confers. But where abuses occur, they are against the public interest because consumers have to pay more, or because the range of goods available to them is reduced.

Product and geographic markets

Since what companies may or may not do depends on whether or not they pass some market share threshold, a great deal depends on the measurement of market share. And in order to calculate market share, one has to define precisely the product market, and the geographic market.

The product market is defined mainly by whether products can be substituted by consumers. The market for soft drinks is clearly different from the market for motor cars, because the two products are not close substitutes. Similarly the market for game shows is different from the market for news programmes. A game show may be an adequate substitute for a soap or a sitcom to the viewer seeking entertainment, but it is not an adequate substitute for a news programme if the viewer wants to find out what has happened today.

The geographic market is also defined by the possibility of substitution. Coca Cola in Ealing is a good substitute for Coca Cola in Acton, and if a local monopolist in Ealing tries to exploit his market power, consumers will simply travel to Acton to buy their Coke. By contrast television programmes in one location are not a good substitute for programmes in another, because the whole point of television is that it is available at the touch of a button in the home. Local monopolies are thus a feature of the media markets worth special attention.

Abusing market power in the media

These simple concepts can be helpful in focusing the debate about concentration in the media markets. The question is what media products are available to a consumer at a particular location. How much market power does any one media company have over the consumer of news in Manchester, Leeds, London etc? How high does the market share have to be before we worry about excessive influence?

If we ask the same question about game shows, we would not be at all worried, from a pluralism standpoint, if one company cornered the entire UK market in this product. We would worry only if the company started charging exorbitant prices for its products. But in that case we might simply refer the company to the Monopolies and Mergers Commission. For many media products, the special concerns about pluralism do not apply, but ordinary competition policy can be used to achieve the desired aims.

These considerations are highly relevant to the debate about sports rights, where companies can earn monopoly rents on the exclusive rights they have secured to certain sporting events. However, if a media controller attempts to do this (e.g. by charging high subscription rates for channels in which exclusive sports coverage is the only serious attraction), then competition law can in principle be invoked to prevent this sort of monopolistic behaviour (though we have yet to see a case of this kind).

Additional regulation to protect pluralism

These examples show that competition policy has an important role to play in the regulation of media markets. But competition policy on its own does not deliver all the desiderata because of the peculiar characteristics of media products and services. Media policy is concerned with ensuring that firms do not exercise excessive 'influence' as well as with preventing abuses of market power and anti-competitive behaviour. To this end, we would suggest three principles to underpin the rules governing media concentration:

(1) The market should be defined by media products, not the means of transmission of those products.

(2) The rules governing the markets in information and opinion should be more tightly drawn than those governing the market in entertainment.

(3) The market should be defined to exclude the public service broadcaster.

The first principle implies that the relevant markets are not the television market, the radio market and the newspaper market, but rather the products transmitted by those means – the game show market, the news market, the market in political comment.

The second principle implies that we should be more worried if a single company has 20 per cent of the market in news than we would be if it had 20 per cent of the market in game shows. The market share required to exert excessive influence may be less than that needed to wield excessive market power.

The third principle is to protect those who rely exclusively on the commercial sector for their information and opinions. Since balance and diversity of views are guaranteed by the terms of the BBC's Charter it would be quite inappropriate to set up a regulatory framework which implied that the BBC itself had excessive influence. The purpose of the framework is to guarantee the same sort of balance and diversity across the commercial sector.

The other issues relating to media concentration, such as the monopoly power (i.e. the power to set prices independently of customers, suppliers and competitors) conferred by control over valuable programme rights or over conditional access, may well raise problems for pluralism but they essentially involve the application of the general competition rules.

And so, at the heart of a successful media ownership policy, there must be clear and practicable definitions of the product and geographic markets which comprise the media. There also need to be easy-to-apply and transparent ways of measuring those markets. The DNH proposals, while setting out the relevant principles, do not resolve these issues.

IV Comments on the DNH proposals

Defining the product market

The White Paper proposes market share thresholds for individual sectors: TV, radio, and newspapers. It also proposes a threshold for the media market as a whole, which is defined as the sum of these three sectors. The weakness of this approach is that it conflates news and opinion output, where pluralism matters greatly, with entertainment programmes, where it matters much less.

The absurdity of defining the product market to include all genres within one medium is illustrated by Table 1 which shows audience ratings for different genres of TV programmes. These data, derived from two weeks of BARB viewing data, show the number of viewing hours for these programmes by terrestrial, cable and satellite television.

Table 1. UK TV audience by genre

Genre	% viewing
Drama	29.2
Film	9.8
Light entertainment	18.2
Children's	7.6
Sport	6.9
Documentary	17.3
News	11.0

Source: BARB (January 1994); LE analysis.

The highest ratings are for drama and light entertainment. News achieves relatively low ratings of 11%. Thus a company which had complete control over all news output, but very low ratings in other genres, would emerge with a low overall market share on the definition of the market proposed in the White Paper. Yet clearly we should worry about the influence exerted by such a company.

If the objective of regulation is to limit the political influence of any one company, the government's proposed product market definition is much too wide. If, on the other hand, the concern is for the market in 'news, information and entertainment' as a whole, then the regulatory approach must take into account the fact that the newspaper, television and radio industries face competition from other suppliers of printed, audio and audio-visual entertainment products.

This is most obvious in the market for filmed entertainment, where the alternatives to watching a film on one of the four main channels include subscribing to a movie channel, buying or renting a video and going to the cinema. Changes in this market have left cinemas, which were once the sole method of distributing filmed entertainment, as a minority outlet, a relatively expensive way of buying early access to new films.

Similarly newspapers, which were once mainly concerned with supplying news and other information, have increasingly entered the market in entertainment (colour supplements, magazine sections etc.). In this market they face competition from a growing range of specialist consumer magazines devoted to every leisure activity under the sun, as well as from the heavily-promoted paperbacks that crowd the shelves of newsagents across the country.

Thus, if the problem that regulation is supposed to address is political influence, then the proposed definition of the market (the total output of press, radio and television) is too broad. But if the problem is excessive commercial influence, especially in the market for entertainment, then the proposed market definition is too narrow.

Table 2. Total UK media market, by revenue, 1993

	Revenue (£m)	%
Terrestrial TV	2930	19.6
Satellite	471	3.2
Radio	556	3.7
National press	2762	18.5
Regional press	2342	15.7
Consumer magazines	1460	9.8
Books	2699	18.1
Cinema	361	2.4
Video rental and sell through	1171	7.9
Theatres	216	1.4
Total	14,968	100.0

Sources: Advertising Statistics Yearbook, ITC Annual Report, BBC Annual Report, BFI Film and TV Handbook, Theatres Management Group, The Bookseller.

Table 2 offers a picture of the broader UK media market. It extends beyond newspapers, television and radio to include pre-recorded video, cinema, books, consumer magazines and the theatre. It could arguably be defined still more broadly, to include pre-recorded and live music; scientific, technical and management journals; the visual arts; electronic on-line services etc.

Geographical market

The DNH's contention that concerns about excessive influence and insufficient competition may arise at national, regional and local levels is incontestable. The aim of regulation is to ensure reasonable diversity and balance in the information and entertainment available in the more than 20 million households across the UK. Some of those homes will always be unreachable by satellite and many others will never be cabled. The main worry, from a pluralism viewpoint, is that a company might acquire excessive influence in a local market through its ownership of both a local newspaper and the local commercial television franchise. Yet, if such a company operated only in one English region, its share of the national media markets would be so small that it would comfortably pass under all the proposed thresholds.

The obvious way of regulating to prevent this is to look at market shares in local markets as well as nationally. The DNH proposes to do this by measuring market shares in each region and by having separate thresholds for the regional market share as well as for the national market share. The regional thresholds are set at a higher level than the national ones – in other words excessive local influence is considered less worrying than excessive national influence.

It is certainly right to regulate at the local level, because local monopolies, especially in television, are absolute in a way that is not true of other products. If the local shop or pub overcharges, most people have the option of travelling further afield. Goods in neighbouring towns are a substitute for the expensive local goods. But this option does not exist for television, the whole point of which is that it is available at the touch of a button in one's own home. So if there is a stream of biased news transmitted in the Manchester area, it is no comfort to the viewer that a more balanced world view is available across the Pennines in Leeds.

Regulation is needed to ensure balance, not just across the country as a whole, but more especially in each region. Taking into account the three components of pluralism – influence, access and content – as well as the provisos about the relative influence, in terms of pluralism, of different information 'genres', it is not obvious why the framework of regulation should be any more tolerant of a local monopoly than of a national monopoly. There is a case for setting the local and national thresholds at the same level.

The unit of measurement

General principles

The influence of a medium of communication depends on a number of different factors. It obviously depends on the number of people it can reach – a newspaper sold to 1 million people will tend to have more influence than one which reaches only 100,000 people. But the fact that a newspaper is bought (something we can measure) does not mean it is read, or read by only one person (readership is much harder to measure than circulation). Moreover, a paper that is read carefully will have more influence than one which is merely skimmed, and while we can use surveys to find out how many people read each newspaper, we cannot know how carefully they read them, or what they read in them. Serious news and political comment competes for the reader's attention with sport, the crossword, the TV listings and the horoscope!

Similarly for a television programme to have any influence, clearly the set must be switched on and tuned to the right channel, which can be measured electronically. With more difficulty we can use surveys to establish who is watching it and for how long. But the degree of attention with which it is being watched is almost impossible to establish.

A third dimension to the problem concerns who is in the audience. A programme or newspaper article that reaches a single person may have a lot more influence than one which reaches a million if the single person happens to be the Prime Minister. Programmes and articles which regularly reach opinion formers and decision makers – chief executives, journalists, Civil Servants and MPs – clearly have influence which cannot be measured just by counting heads.

These considerations suggest that the influence of any medium of communication is a complex function of the number of people it regularly reaches, who those people are, and how attentive to the output they are. That, in turn, suggests that there is unlikely to be a single measure which gives us an accurate indication of influence. Audience measures tell us the number of people reached. Time use may offer some guide to the *amount* (but not the quality) of attention paid. Revenue figures help us to gauge the importance attached collectively by viewers, readers, listeners and advertisers to what is printed or transmitted.

Ultimately the judgement about the influence of a particular medium is going to be qualitative. The media regulator will clearly need a great deal of information, extracted from a wide range of indicators to help him/her decide if the influence of a particular company in the media market is a cause for concern (just as the Chancellor of the Exchequer is given a huge amount of information from different statistical sources to help him decide if inflationary pressures are sufficient to justify a rise in interest rates). In neither case can we hope to find a set of statistical indicators which will relieve the decision maker of responsibility.

Audience based measures

The problem of measuring influence is not a new one. The advertising industry has been grappling with it for decades. The amount advertisers are prepared to pay per column inch of newspaper, or per 30 seconds of television/radio airtime, depends on the number of readers, viewers and listeners. For this reason audited measures of newspaper circulation, television and radio audience are widely available.

We can thus measure market shares within each medium relatively easily and accurately. We know the total number of newspapers sold, and we can measure the market share of each newspaper group relative to this yardstick. Similarly, we know the total number of television sets tuned to each channel on a regular basis, and we can again measure the share of each television company relative to this total.

Arguably, the influence of newspapers depends more on the number of readers than on the number of copies sold. And the influence of television programmes depends more on the number of viewers than on the number of sets tuned. For this reason the hard data on copies sold and the reliable sample data on sets tuned needs to be supplemented by survey data on readership per newspaper and number of viewers per set.

This approach will give us market shares based on the number of people reached by each medium. But there is no obvious solution to the problem of creating an *overall* market share. If a particular company has 10 per cent of the television market and 20 per cent of the newspaper market and nothing in radio, what is its share of the total media market? We need to find some robust and objective method of constructing a weighted average of these three market shares to arrive at a single figure for the media market as a whole.

Weighted audience share

The British Media Industry Group (BMIG)[2] has proposed a solution to this problem. Their approach uses audience figures to calculate market shares for television and radio, and circulation figures to calculate the market share for printed material (newspapers). They then construct an average share of the overall media market by assigning weights of 1 to television, national and regional newspapers, and 0.5 to radio. They put forward two arguments to justify these weights:

·   radio is a 'secondary' medium, one which people can consume while involved in other activities; and

·   radio has a low level of news and current affairs.

The chief merit of the BMIG approach, the results of which are shown in Table 3, is that it uses a measure of market share for each medium which is appropriate to that medium. However, there are two problems with its proposal, one minor and one major. The minor problem is that it is somewhat inconsistent to measure shares in the printed media market on the basis of circulation (which is essentially a household based measure) while using audience figures (which count individual viewers) for television and radio. It would have been more consistent to use newspaper readership – rather than circulation – as the basis of comparison.

But this matters much less than the other problem with the BMIG approach, which is the arbitrary nature of the weighting system. It is probably right to assign a lower weight to radio than to the other media. The influence of a medium for a particular consumer is likely to be greater the higher the level of effort made in consumption. So a 'secondary' medium could well have a lower level of influence.

However, there is no objective justification for the arbitrary figure of 50 per cent, especially as it is far from obvious that radio does have a low level of news and current affairs compared to other media. Capital Radio FM, for example, has regular news bulletins as well as other programmes devoted to commentary and opinions. This is a pattern followed by many radio stations. Furthermore, there are some radio

---

2. BMIG, *A New Approach to Cross-media Ownership* 1995.

programmes that are widely considered to be as influential as any output on television or in the newspapers.

Table 3. Media concentration (TV, newspapers, and radio) under audience share analysis 1993/94

Media group	% share of audience
BBC	19.7
News International	10.6
(ITV Network)*	9.4
Daily Mail Trust	7.8
Mirror Group Newspapers	7.6
United Newspapers	5.7
Carlton Communications	3.1
Channel 4	2.9
Total as a % of newspaper, TV & radio markets	57.4

* LE estimate using BMIG methodology.
In this table, as in most that follow, we have computed a figure for the market share of the ITV Network. Although the companies which make up the network are commercially independent of each other, they jointly own the Network Centre and ITN, co-produce regional programmes (including news) and therefore exercise editorial control *collectively* over a substantial part of ITV output.
Source: BMIG, February 1995.

Each medium will use its own measure of circulation/ listenership/audience share. There are obvious attractions in the construction of a single measure of market share based on a weighted average of the shares in each medium. But there does need to be some objective basis for the choice of weights. The BMIG falls down on the arbitrary nature of its weighting system.

Time-based measures

A study by Arthur Andersen[3] proposed using time spent consuming media as a measure of influence. The beauty of this approach is that time use is a common denominator across all the media. So if there is any validity in the basic proposition that the influence of a medium of communication is proportional to the time taken to absorb the message, the time use measure dispenses with the need for a weighting system. Time can be used as the measure of market share in each medium, and by simply summing the time use across all the media we can calculate an overall market share. Table 4 shows the results of applying this methodology.

However there are major difficulties with this measure. According to the Arthur Andersen report, the amount of time spent watching television is nearly seven times as great as that spent reading national newspapers. But this figure may substantially exaggerate the impact of television compared to the printed medium, on both qualitative and quantitative grounds.

National newspapers have an impact that lasts far longer than the time spent reading them. Newspaper headlines are seen by, and influence, millions of people who do not buy or read the papers whose front pages they dominate. It is the

---
3. Arthur Andersen *UK Media Concentration* 1994.

newspaper headlines that largely determine the current affairs agenda at the start of each day, and that influence persists even though new sources of information are obtained from television in the evening.

Table 4. Media concentration under time-use analysis, 1993

Media group	% of time spent 'consuming'
BBC	44.1
(ITV Network)*	25.4
Carlton	6.9
Channel 4	6.2
Granada	4.1
Capital Radio	3.4
News International	3.4

* LE estimate using Arthur Andersen methodology;
Source: Arthur Andersen 1994.

Consumer expenditure also gives an indication of the relative value placed on the media. For the price of a broadsheet newspaper (50 pence per day prior to the price cutting of 1994/5), a viewer would be able to obtain the basic satellite service plus two premium channels, which costs around £17 per month.[4] The national newspaper proposition attracts 14 million people each day compared with only 3 million people paying for satellite television services.

This comparison may be flawed – because the satellite services have to compete with free television to a much greater extent than national newspapers compete with regional and 'free sheet' newspapers. However, it does reinforce the view that the relative value placed on national newspapers (and hence their influence) may be much greater than is suggested by the relative amount of time spent reading them compared with watching television.

Weighted time use

Another way of measuring relative influence is to examine the behaviour of advertisers. For example, advertisers buy space in national newspapers and time on television because of beliefs concerning the influence of those media. Advertisers were prepared to spend £1.2 billion on national newspapers and £2.6 billion on television advertisements in 1993.[5] So although television is over eight times more important than national newspapers in terms of time use, advertisers only regard it as roughly twice as important.

Both newspaper and television advertisers recognise that it is not just the number of viewers, listeners and readers that matters. It is who they are. The *Independent* is a serious newspaper read by many influential people in business, the City, Whitehall and Westminster. So although space in the *Independent* is cheaper than space in the *Sun* (because there are far fewer readers), the cost per reader of advertising in the Independent is much higher than that of advertising in the *Sun*.

4. Independent Newspapers, *BSkyB Prospectus 1994*.

5. Advertising Association, *Advertising Statistics Yearbook 1994*.

This is illustrated by the advertising rate cards shown in Table 5. The amount that advertisers are prepared to pay to reach the highly influential FT reader would buy access to no less than fourteen *Sun* readers.

Table 5. Advertising ratecard costs of selected national newspapers

Newspaper	£/page	£/000 adult readers
The Sun	28,000	2.84
Daily Mail	22,680	4.80
Independent	14,000	12.20
Daily Telegraph	34,500	12.71
Sunday Times	47,000	13.28
Financial Times	29,568	39.69

Source: BRAD 1994.

In the same way, advertising slots in television programmes that are likely to attract a higher proportion of ABC1s will be more highly valued, on a cost per viewer basis, than slots in programmes delivering a large proportion of C2DEs.

These considerations reinforce the attractions of advertising data as a measure of influence. The relationship between money and influence is imperfect, but money-based measures do at least take into account, in a way that head counts cannot, the fact that the influence of any medium depends on who it reaches, as well as how many it reaches.

However, although advertising expenditure gives us some clue as to the relative influence of radio and television compared to the press, it is hard to construct a robust statistical measure of relative influence, because print is bought by the column inch or page part, whereas radio and television is bought by the second. It is also extremely difficult to be sure of comparing like with like. Television is much more influential at 8 pm, when the audiences are huge, than in the day time. Space in newspapers may be more influential on some pages than others. These points must be borne in mind when making comparison based on simple averages.

Table 6. Relative advertising costs, 1993

Medium	£ per hour* per adult
TV	0.71
Radio	0.13
Newspapers	2.94
Cinema	1.72
Magazines	2.08

* of viewing, listening to or reading advertisements;
Source: Advertising Association Handbook, Arthur Andersen and LE analysis.

Table 6 shows the results of marrying time use data with advertising cost data. We know, from time use data, the number of hours per week spent consuming each medium in the average household. We can multiply up by the number of households to estimate total hours. If the total advertising spend of each medium is divided by the total numbers of hours spent consuming each medium, we have an implicit price, in pounds per person per hour, that an advertiser using each medium is prepared to spend to reach its audience.

The exercise is heroic because, in order to arrive at a figure for the cost *per hour* of advertising in newspapers and magazines, we have to make an assumption about the proportion of the time devoted to these products that is spent looking at the advertisements. We assume that the proportion is the same as for television.

The results shown in Table 6 are that advertisers in the print media are in general prepared to pay 4 times as much per hour to reach their audiences. These ratios would be even larger if, as seems likely, the amount of time spent reading advertisements in the press is less than the 7 minutes per hour of commercial television advertising.

We can use these figures to create a weighting system, in which time spent reading the press is valued at 4 times the value of time spent watching television, while time spent listening to the radio is valued at 0.2. We have used our database on time use by media company to calculate the market shares with and without the weighting factors. Our figures for simple time use in Table 7, it should be noted, differ from those shown in Table 4 (calculated by Arthur Andersen), largely because of the way we have calculated companies' shares of TV viewing and radio listening.

Table 7. Media concentration (newspapers, TV & radio) under time use, 1993

Media group	% share: simple time use	% share: weighted time use
BBC	44.9	30.4
(ITV network)	25.4	24.3
Carlton	8.0	7.7
Granada	5.8	5.5
Channel 4	5.6	5.4
News International	4.5	12.0
Capital Radio	3.9	0.7
MAI	3.8	3.6
Mirror Group	1.8	7.1

Source: Arthur Andersen 1994; RAJAR 1994; Advertising Association; LE analysis.

Table 7 shows, using weighted as against unweighted time-use measures, a substantial reduction in the market shares for the BBC and Capital Radio, as one would expect given their strong positions in the radio market. The position of the TV-based companies changes very little. However newspaper companies have much larger market shares, and in particular News International becomes much the strongest commercial company.

These complex calculations go some way to overcoming the difficulties and shortcomings of the pure time-based approach, but the resulting measure is far from transparent and relies on some contestable assumptions. The contrast between the weighted and unweighted time use measures illustrates the fragility of any calculations of this sort and shows how elusive a satisfactory measure is.

Revenue

Table 8 shows market shares based on *revenue*, which is the unit of measurement most heavily used in competition policy. It is clearly related to economic power. It has the advantage that it does not require calculation of the 'media exchange rates' in aggregating sectors. Revenue is a good overall measure of the willingness of advertisers to transmit, and of audiences to receive via a particular medium. It is a measure which reflects not just the number of viewers/listeners/readers, but also the amount they are prepared to pay, which in turn reflects the value, and hence the influence, of the medium.

Table 8. Media market shares (TV, newspaper and radio) under revenue measures, 1993

Company	%
BBC	17.5
(ITV network)	16.0
News International	11.6
Daily Mail	6.5
Mirror Group	6.0
United Newspapers	5.7
Pearson	5.3
Carlton	5.3
Granada	4.1
Channel 4	3.6
Conrad Black Investments	3.3
MAI	2.2
Guardian Group	1.6

Sources: BBC Annual Report, Advertising Association; Zenith UK Media Yearbook 1994; ITC; LE analysis.

In the media, as in many other industries, a company which has a larger share of revenues is likely to invest a larger portion of its resources in improving the quality of its product in order to stay ahead of its competitors. If the investment is well judged, the improvement in product feeds through into higher market share. In the media industry the scope for spectacular mistakes makes the link between re-investment and market share more tenuous than in other industries. But ultimately the link between the resources a company commands, and its ability to retain and influence audiences, must hold.

However, the relationship in the media between revenues and influence is far from straightforward and varies across the different media. Consider the case of a newspaper which cuts its cover price. It will increase its circulation and hence its influence, but may reduce its revenue (depending on the elasticity of sales, and the importance of advertising revenue with respect to the cover price). A powerful newspaper proprietor with deep pockets, who was determined to get his message across at any cost, could simultaneously reduce his market share and increase his influence by reducing the cover price of his newspapers.

By contrast, the revenue earned by a commercial free-to-air television channel, which comes predominantly from the sale of advertising, may be a better measure of influence, since success consists in putting on programmes that large numbers of people (or smaller numbers of high-spenders) want to watch. The larger the audiences, the more advertisers will pay for commercial slots, the greater the revenue and the greater the influence.

Revenue-weighted audience shares

It can be argued that total influence of a medium is a function of both the size of the audience and its quality. The size is picked up by audience share measures, and the quality by revenue measures. This is because advertisers pay more to reach a rich and influential audience, and because those who pay to receive a medium probably also pay more attention to what they receive.

Of course a media controller bent on exerting political influence, may be particularly interested in the *number* of people influenced, independent of their socio-economic weight, since there is no difference in the value of a rich person's and a poor person's vote. On the other hand, we live in a representative democracy, with the power devolved from the masses to an oligarchic elite (MPs and Civil Servants). The most effective way to influence policy decisions is to target that elite directly, as the growth of the lobbying industry shows.

For these reasons it is interesting to compute an alternative weighted average of market shares across the four media sectors, using as the weights the share of each medium in total turnover of the media. This measure has the advantages of the BMIG approach, and arguably avoids the serious disadvantage, which is the arbitrary nature of the weighting system. Table 9 shows the revenue weights for each media sector.

Table 9. Revenue weightings by media sector, 1993

	Revenue (£m)	Ratio
National newspapers	2762	0.81
TV	3401	1
Radio	556	0.16
Regional newspapers	2342	0.69

Source: BBC Annual Report 1993/4; Advertising Association; ITC annual report; LE analysis.

We calculate overall market shares as follows. For each sector, we calculate the audience share of each media group. We then multiply this audience share by the appropriate revenue weighting factor to determine the 'revenue-weighted audience share points' for each media group in that sector. For each company we add together the points coming from each of the media sectors. We calculate market share as the number of points for each company divided by the total number of media points.

Table 10 shows the results of these calculations. We have used our media database to recalculate the shares with and without the revenue weights. The salient feature of this approach is that it gives a much lower weight to radio, and a slightly lower weight to the press, than the BMIG weightings. However it turns out that the results are not very different.

Table 10. Media market share (TV, newspaper and radio) using audience share, 1993

Company	% using revenue weights	% using BMIG weights
BBC	19.2	19.6
News International	12.8	11.3
(ITV Network)	11.3	9.4
Daily Mirror	8.3	7.4
Daily Mail	7.5	7.2
United Newspapers	6.4	6.1
Channel 4	4.0	3.3
Carlton	3.7	3.1
Granada	2.8	2.3
Pearson	2.6	2.6
Guardian Media	2.3	2.3
Conrad Black	1.8	1.6
Capital Radio	0.9	1.9

Source: Zenith Media Yearbook 1994; RAJAR 1994; BARB Jan 1994; LE analysis.

Reach of information and opinion

A final option, which is in many ways the simplest of all, is to define the market for information and opinion as the total number of people in a given time period who read any newspaper plus the total number of people who view any news or current affairs programme. The share of any medium would then be given by the number of people it reached in a given period, divided by the total number in the market in that period. Table 11 shows the results of these calculations.

The advantages of measuring market share in terms of reach/readership are:

·   it involves no 'exchange rate';

·   unlike audience share, which only measures past performance, reach/readership provides an indicator of likely *potential* influence;

·   it is immune to temporary influences on audience/readership, such as a particularly popular TV programme, presenter or promotional effort (e.g. bingo); and

- it is easily extendable to other media products and services, such as books or on-line services.

Table 11. UK media market share (TV, newspaper and radio) using reach, 1993

Company	% reach
BBC	26.0
(ITV network)	9.6
Channel 4	8.5
News International	7.2
Daily Mail	5.7
Daily Mirror	5.1
United Newspapers	4.6
Carlton	3.2
Pearson	2.5
Granada	2.4
Guardian Media	2.0
Capital Radio	1.5
Conrad Black	1.0

Source: BBC Facts and Figures 1993/4; Zenith UK Media Yearbook 1994; RAJAR March 1994; LE analysis.

The main disadvantage of the reach/readership based share is that, to a greater extent than even audience share, it fails to reflect the *intensity* of consumption and it is even more difficult with reach than audience share to distinguish between the consumption of different genres of information or between different classes of consumer. The application of a reach-based measure may also, in time, come to overstate the market importance of the public service broadcasters, BBC, Channel 4 and S4C, who are tending to target reach.

Market shares under different units of measurement

Table 12 shows the results of applying the methodologies discussed above to the 1993 UK media market.

The different measures produce very different outcomes and variations of up to 1,200 per cent (in the case of Capital Radio) depending on the measure adopted. The revenue measure, used in isolation, may overstate the influence of the press and understate that of radio. Reach may overstate the impact of the public service broadcasters. Simple time use may exaggerate the importance of television and radio. The weighted time use and audience share measures suffer from arbitrariness.

Summary of measurement options

Table 13 summarises our assessment of the different units of measurement.

The picture which emerges from the comparison of the various approaches to measuring media market shares is that no single measure will capture all the dimensions required to gauge influence (and, by extension, access and diversity of content). Some kind of weighting – which will inevitably involve a degree of arbitrariness – will always be required and, with the exception of revenue and reach,

Table 12. Market shares of top 12 companies for different units of measurement

	Reach	Revenue	Simple time use	Weighted time use	Audience share (BMIG weights)	Audience share (revenue weights)
BBC	26.0%	17.5%	44.9%	30.4%	19.6%	19.2%
(ITV Network)	9.6%	16.0%	25.4%	24.3%	9.4%	11.3%
Channel 4	8.5%	3.6%	5.6%	5.4%	3.3%	4.0%
News International	7.2%	11.6%	4.5%	12.0%	11.3%	12.8%
Daily Mail	5.7%	6.5%	1.2%	4.6%	7.2%	7.5%
Daily Mirror	5.1%	6.0%	1.8%	7.1%	7.4%	8.3%
United Newspapers	4.6%	5.7%	1.1%	4.5%	6.1%	6.4%
Carlton	3.2%	5.3%	8.0%	7.7%	3.1%	3.7%
Pearson	2.5%	5.3%	1.2%	1.7%	2.6%	2.6%
Granada	2.4%	4.1%	5.8%	5.5%	2.3%	2.8%
Guardian Media	2.0%	1.6%	0.2%	0.8%	2.3%	2.3%
Capital Radio	1.5%	0.3%	3.9%	0.7%	1.9%	0.9%
Conrad Black	1.0%	3.3%	0.4%	1.8%	1.6%	1.8%
Share of 12 companies	69.7%	70.8%	78.7%	82.1%	6.8%	72.4%

Notes: *Reach*: proportion of *number* of viewers, listeners and readers of all media products in a given time period (week); *Revenue*: share of revenue of all media companies in a given year; *Simple time use*: proportion of time spent consuming media products in a given period; *Weighted time use*: proportion of time spent consuming media products, where time is weighted according to the value placed on it by advertisers in the different media; *Audience share (BMIG weights)*: share of each media market computed as proportion of number of viewers, listeners, readers respectively and then a weighted average taken using weights of 1 for press and television, 0.5 for radio; *Audience share (revenue weight)*: as above, except that weights are based on the revenue share of each medium.

so will an 'exchange rate'. The preferred approach must be simple, avoid arbitrary assumptions, be susceptible to extension to media products and services in addition to television, newspapers and radio, and be forward-looking. In practice, it may be impossible to define a measure which can be applied universally (to all media) in every circumstance.

Table 13. Assessment of market share measurement units put forward to date

Measurement unit	Advantages	Disadvantages
Time use	No need for exchange rate	Loose connection between time use and influence
Weighted time use	More closely related to influence than time use alone	Heroic assumptions required to make measure work
Audience shares	Easily measured	Head count ignores fact that some audiences are more influential. Doesn't capture relative influence of different sectors
Revenue	No need for an exchange rate. Revenue provides the money to make programmes which attract more viewers. Captures fact that more influential audiences generate more revenue	Two-way relationship between revenue and influence both indirect and variable
Revenue-weighted audience share	Uses revenue as an objective weighting system. Combines advantages of revenue and audience measures	Still suffers from unreliable link between revenue and influence
Reach	Potentially the simplest measure, involving no 'exchange rate'. Relates directly to democratic (i.e. undifferentiated mass) outcomes	Fails to capture intensity of consumption

V Conclusions

A framework for media ownership regulation

We would suggest that a clear definition of what is meant by pluralism must underpin any attempt to regulate media ownership. We have suggested three key elements of pluralism: restricting the influence of any one organisation, guaranteeing access and fostering diversity of content. The aim of regulation of market share is primarily to restrict influence, but it ought, within a general competition framework, to provide the necessary – though not sufficient – condition for access and for content diversity.

In order to determine how to measure market share, it is first necessary to say precisely what we mean by influence. We have suggested two possible definitions: political influence, and the much wider influence in the print and audio-visual industries as a whole. The first refers to news and current affairs, possibly including the arts. The second refers to all printed information and audio-visual entertainment.

There are two different product markets corresponding to these different definitions of influence: the market in news and current affairs; and the market in printed information and audio-visual entertainment. These are the markets, extending beyond television, radio and newspapers, in which the shares of different companies should be measured by the regulator. There are strong arguments for excluding public service broadcasters from the definition of the market, since there are already detailed regulations guaranteeing the pluralism of PSB output.

Careful thought must go into determining what is/are the relevant market/markets. For the regulator, the clearer the focus the better. This might lead to adopting narrow market definitions, but applying narrow definitions may not be practical given the market data available. Since, therefore, the regulator will tend, in making judgements about the market, to look at the broad media sector, he or she must be allowed to exercise discretion over the appropriate measurements to use to determine the ability of any media owner to influence the news agenda, say, or opinion more broadly.

If these problems can successfully be negotiated, there can then be established thresholds on the market shares of individual *companies* of the relevant media product market. There may also be a case for imposing a threshold for any company's share of each individual medium, if it can be shown (for example) that those who get their information from television or radio, are a totally different sector of the population than those who get it from the press. The case for thresholds for each medium is then the same as the case for thresholds in each locality. Excessive influence is bad, whether it is concentrated locally or by medium of transmission.

Unit of measurement

Once the product market has been defined, there are many different possible ways of measuring share of the market. In our view each one of these measures conveys some important information about the markets and the degree of influence of each company within them but none is so perfect or unambiguous to displace the need for the regulator's judgement. The media regulator will undoubtedly want to compute all of these measures and examine them carefully before coming to any conclusion about the excessive influence of any one company. An over-reliance on the measures may lead to unrealisable or flawed policies.

The use of a combination of measures is essential since no single measure captures both the quantity and quality of consumption which will tend to determine the degree of influence exerted and the extent of access and of content diversity offered. But it is the duty of a regulator, in the final analysis, to deploy any and all measurement approaches he or she deems necessary to build up a complete picture of the market and the actions required to ensure the outcomes the regulation aims to achieve.

Annexe: Calculating relative influence using advertising weights

In Table 14 we have obtained the relative advertising costs for TV, radio, news-papers, cinema and magazines. The unit we use is that of spend (£) per one hour of watching (or listening to, or reading) advertisements per person.

Table 14. Analysis of relative advertising costs (1993)

		TV	Radio	National and regional newspapers	Cinema	Consumer magazines
	Population					
1	UK adult population	46,957	46,957	46,957	46,957	46,957
	Advertising data					
2	Advertising expend (£m) 1993	2,605	194	2,935	49	475
3	Assumed % Advertising minutes/hour	11.7	11.7	11.7	11.7	11.7
	Time use					
4	Time use per person per week (non BBC) in hours	12.9	5.1	3.5	0.1	0.8
5	Time use per person per year (hours)	672.6	265.9	182.5	5.2	41.7
6	Time spent on advertising per person per year (hours)	78.5	31.1	21.3	0.6	4.9
	Calculations					
7	£m advertising spend per one hour advertisement watching (total population)	33.2	6.3	137.8	80.5	97.6
	Result					
8	£ advertising spend per one hour viewing advertisements per capita	0.71	0.13	2.94	1.72	2.08
9	Ratio compared to TV	1	0.19	4.15	2.43	2.94

(1) Source: OPCS; (2) Source: Zenith UK Media Yearbook; (3) ITC regulations stipulate a maximum average of 7 minutes of advertising per hour; (4) Arthur Andersen 1994; (5) row 4 × 365/7; (6) row 3 × row 5; (7) row 2 /row 6 and (8) row 7/row 1.

We have made the heroic assumption that people spend the same time on advertisements for each hour of reading newspapers or magazines, as for each hour of viewing or listening to commercial television or radio. Then the analysis proceeds as follows:

- We calculate the advertising cost to reach the entire population for one hour for a particular medium. We divide total advertising spend per year on a medium (2) by the number of hours of advertisements per year that an individual adult watches for that medium (6).

- We obtain the advertising cost per capita by dividing the advertising cost for the whole population (7) by the size of the population (1).

The Cross Media Revolution: Ownership and Control

i